JESUS
on
TRIAL

KEL RICHARDS

❁ MATTHIAS MEDIA

Jesus on Trial
© Matthias Media, 2001

Matthias Media
PO Box 225
Kingsford NSW 2032
Australia
Ph: (02) 9663 1478   International ph: +61-2-9663 1478
Fax (02) 9663 3265   International fax: +61-2-9663 3265
Email: info@matthiasmedia.com.au
Internet: www.matthiasmedia.com.au

Distributed in South Africa by:
Christian Book Discounters
Ph: (021) 685 3663
Email: peter@christianbooks.co.za

Distributed in the United Kingdom by:
The Good Book Company
Ph: (020) 8942 0880
Email: admin@thegoodbook.co.uk

Unless otherwise indicated, Scripture taken from the HOLY BIBLE, NEW
INTERNATIONAL VERSION. Copyright © 1973, 1978, 1984 International
Bible Society. Used by permission of Zondervan Bible Publishers.

ISBN 1 876326 40 9

Cover design and typesetting by Joy Lankshear Design Pty Ltd.
Printed in Australia.

Contents

Introduction

JURY DUTY

*H*ave you ever been called up for jury duty? No? Well, it has happened to me. In the part of the world where I live the process works like this. You receive a letter saying that you are on the jury list. It also tells you what excuses might get you out of it (there are not many) and how you're to find out when you're needed.

This involves making a phone call on a Sunday night to a recorded message that recites the numbers of the lists that are being called up. If you discover that your list is not needed on the morrow (as happened to me once) you can then relax— until next time. Because there will be a next time.

Another letter comes, once again full of dire warnings of the consequences if you don't do your duty as a citizen and sit in judgement on another citizen. Once again on the Sunday night you call the recorded number, but this time the group that includes you is required to turn up.

This means arriving at the central court building before nine o'clock on Monday morning, being sat in a court room while the roll is called (it's a bit like being back in school again), and then being hustled into a large jury waiting room that has all the style and panache of a railway station. Here you can a collect a form asking to be excused from jury duty. On the one occasion I was there, I duly completed my form and handed it in, and then waited to see if I would be released or required. As it turned out, I was let off.

But what if I had served that day?

I would have sat in a jury box with a bunch of other total strangers (known to the law as 'my peers') and heard a judge instruct me to listen carefully to the evidence and the arguments, and, putting aside emotion, prejudice and speculation, reach a determination as to the matters of fact in the case.

And that is what I am charging you to do.

I will bring before you the evidence as it exists with respect to Jesus—who he was and what happened to him. And just like a member of a jury, I am inviting you to put aside emotion, prejudice and speculation. I ask you to consider the weight of the evidence, and the balance of probabilities, and determine whether the facts are proved, if not beyond all possible doubt, at least beyond reasonable doubt.

Why would you take up such an invitation? One reason is this: there is a bunch of people—a minority, to be sure, but a bunch nonetheless—who take Jesus very seriously indeed. These are people who appear, on the whole, to be perfectly normal in every other way, but who believe that the Creator God of the Universe has visited this planet in the form of a person known as Jesus of Nazareth.

A quite extraordinary belief, on the face of it. How to account for this? Are all of these people congenital idiots? Are they thoughtlessly doing what their parents told them to do when they were mere infants? Do they suffer from some deep psychosis?

These, and other explanations, have been offered. Clearly, none of them will do since this crowd includes poets, scientists, engineers, doctors, lawyers and any number of other intelligent and reasonably balanced persons.

So, members of the jury, what do these people see that the majority miss? That is part of what you are called to pass judgement upon.

THE KEY QUESTION

*L*adies and Gentlemen of the jury (enjoy this bit, you don't often get addressed by old fashioned courtesy titles these days) the question before you is perhaps the single most important question in the world: did Jesus come back from the dead?

The possibility is one that our world really doesn't like to seriously consider. "Not an option", many people will say with a careless wave of the hand.

When Andrew Lloyd Webber and Tim Rice wrote the musical *Jesus Christ, Superstar* they ended the show with Jesus still in the tomb. They looked at what the earliest historical documents (in the New Testament part of the Bible) say about Jesus and decided there was no way they could stage what they read. Instead, they decided to tell their story through the eyes of Judas, the one who betrayed Jesus to the authorities. And Judas committed suicide before Jesus came back from the dead, so that removed the embarrassment of having to deal with that prickly issue.

But it's the most important question all of us can face.

Because all of us are condemned to death. From the moment we are born we are heading down a one way road towards the grave. We spend our lives suppressing the thought, but it is the truth—the ugly truth. Now, if death has been conquered once, by Jesus, there may be good news in that for all us. The possibility is raised that we, too, may survive death, and survive it well. This possibility makes the question a big one for the whole world.

Some years ago Professor C. E. M. Joad was Professor of Philosophy at London University. He was asked, on a BBC radio program: "If you could meet any person from the past and ask just one question, whom would you meet and what question would you ask?". Joad replied, "I would meet Jesus Christ and ask him—'Did you or did you not rise from the dead?'". At the time Professor Joad was not a believer, and yet he could see the importance of the question. (Later in his life Professor Joad did, in fact, become a Christian.)

There is no shortage of people prepared to say that Jesus did *not* come back from the dead.

Some of them are bishops, and some are professors. They lay their reputations on the line and talk about what they call 'the myth of the resurrection'. Should we just take their word for it?

Well, we can't. In a court of law that would involve taking 'hearsay' evidence—or 'second best evidence' as it is sometimes called. And your task, members of the jury, is to consider the best evidence, the first-hand evidence, for or against this remarkable claim that is made with respect to Jesus.

The very earliest believers, the first followers of Jesus, knew how important this claim was. Their story is recorded in a section of the New Testament part of the Bible called "Acts". In that book, a volume that appears to be carefully researched history written by a Greek doctor named Luke, there are summaries of thirteen early sermons or talks. The one fact that is common to all of them is this claim that Jesus came back from the dead.

What they said was, "God has raised this Jesus to life, and we are all witnesses of the fact" (Acts 2:32). And they make it perfectly clear that without a risen, living Jesus they would have given up and gone home. In one letter between those early Christians are these words: "If Christ has not been raised, your faith is futile" (1 Corinthians 15:17). In other words, either Jesus is back again, and in business again, in business permanently, or there is no faith to follow.

❧

A UNIQUE CLAIM

*F*or those members of the jury inclined to shrug their shoulders and mutter, "Well, all religions make odd claims from time to time", it is important to point out that this claim is unique. And that makes it special.

At some point in any court case, the counsel is likely to tell the members of the jury that this or that point is the key one, or the critical one, and they are to pay special attention to it. Likewise, the judge in his summing up, is likely to point out to the jury the one or two key points upon which the truth of the whole case turns.

Well, this claim is that sort of point. When the claim is made that Jesus came back from the dead, a very special sort of claim is being made. It is a claim that underlines the differences between different religions, for no other religion makes the same claim.

No Buddhist ever claimed that Buddha came back from the dead. No Confucian ever claimed that Confucius came back from the dead. No Muslim ever claimed that Mohammed came back from the dead. In fact, according to tradition, Mohammed died on the 8th of June, AD 632, at the age of 61. His tomb still lies in the city of Medina, in Saudi Arabia, where it is visited by thousands of Muslims every year. There is no tomb containing the corpse of Jesus for Christians to visit. There is, it's true, a church built at the site where tradition says that Jesus' tomb was—but it was an empty tomb.

Faced with this claim, some people assume they don't even have to consider it seriously. There is a clear pattern over thousands of years of human history: people who die stay dead.

Therefore (they reason), Jesus did not come back the dead, it's ridiculous to even investigate it, get on to something else.

But that is much too careless and much too hasty.

Strange, unlikely and unpredictable things do happen on rare occasions. And if this particular strange and unlikely thing really did happen on this particular rare and special occasion, then it deserves some attention, and it probably means something significant. I once read about an American green keeper at a golf course who had been struck by lightning three times. On each occasion he had been burnt, but not killed. (If I had bothered to keep the newspaper clipping I could have given you chapter and verse on this man.) Anyway, it's no response to such a report to simply mutter, "Lightning never strikes the same place twice", as if that dealt with it.

It's not my place to tell you what to conclude: that is your role, Ladies and Gentlemen of the jury. However, it is my role to tell you not to dismiss anything before you have considered the evidence, and to keep an open mind on the crucial issues until you have examined the witnesses. In the end, you must settle this vital, all-important question for yourself: did Jesus come back from the dead?

THE STANDARD OF PROOF

*P*erhaps I should, before getting into the substance of the matter, pause to explain to you members of the jury how courts and trials generally proceed. Many different sorts of disputes come before many different courts. Some of them are highly specialized courts.

The most basic division is between criminal and civil courts. In criminal courts the authorities bring a criminal charge against a person (or a group of people); while in a civil case one person brings a legal action against another (or against a company or a council or whatever). When you sue your neighbour, that's a civil action (although it's not a very civil thing to do!), but when you are charged with dangerous driving, that's a criminal action.

In a criminal matter there will be a judge whose task is twofold: to see that the law is obeyed and to pass sentence on the convicted. There will also be a lawyer, or team of lawyers, for each side—the prosecution and the defence. In the jury box at a criminal trial will be twelve ordinary citizens chosen at random.

Some civil trials are heard before a judge alone, and some before a judge and a smaller jury, perhaps of only four people. The role of the jury is to decide what lawyers call 'matters of fact'— that is, to make a pronouncement on what actually happened.

Now the matter before us—who Jesus is and what happened to him—is going to be a civil matter, not a criminal matter.

No one is being charged here with a criminal offence. Instead, there are two parties contending over the truth in this particular instance. Presenting the case for the prosecution (called the 'complainant' in a civil case) will be someone else—someone who argues that what Christians believe about Jesus is a load of old rope. My role is to present the case for the 'respondent' (that means the defence)—to show that believers have good reasons for being believers, and for believing as they do.

So, here we are in a civil court, that mob over there arguing the complainant's case (sometimes I think this world is full of people arguing the complainant's case—movies, newspaper articles, books, pop songs and magazines so often seem to spend their time mocking and ridiculing belief); and over here, at the defence table, me and a lot of scraps of paper as I try to keep my mind, and my arguments, in something roughly resembling logical order.

You, of course, are sitting in the jury box, and in that position you need to understand what lawyers call the 'standard of proof'.

A leading British text book on evidence states: "The standard of proof required in civil cases is generally expressed as proof on the 'balance of probabilities'. If the evidence is such that the jury can say, 'We think it more probable than not', the burden is discharged, but if the probabilities are equal, it is not".

So, in considering who Jesus is and what happened to him and so on, we must apply the same 'standard of proof'. We must ask ourselves, in the light of the evidence, and the arguments, what is *the balance of probabilities*?

We must keep our minds open until we have all the data to decide. That is to say, we must be unbiased. You mustn't be like the foreman of the jury who, when asked to deliver the verdict, said: "Seven of us find the prisoner guilty as charged; three us of find him guilty as all get out; and two of us found him guilty the minute we set eyes on him!".

But with a big, difficult question such as 'Did Jesus come back from the dead?', being unbiased and having no prejudice is far from easy. There was a book written by a Frenchman to disprove the resurrection of Jesus from the dead that began by announcing that the author didn't believe in miracles, and, therefore, the resurrection was not possible.

Such as attitude would not be tolerated in a court of law. We must be as unbiased as we can in examining the evidence.

❧

THE MEANING OF
THE CLAIM

*T*he big word is 'resurrection', and it means that Jesus came back from the dead. But in what sense? What does it mean, exactly? Does it just mean that after Jesus' body was killed his spirit went on without a body? No, it doesn't mean that. Death is physical, and the conquest of death by Jesus is also said to be physical.

The Bible says that Jesus was raised from death with a physical body, but a body that was more than physical, more than the old body in which he had died. It still had the marks, the appearance, of the old body, but it had other capacities as well. It is described as a 'spiritual body'—but it was no ghost. It was solid enough to see, and touch, and handle fish and frying pans. A wonderful change had taken place. Jesus was clearly the same person, and yet in other ways not the same.

There is a book on this subject called *Raised Immortal*, and that title captures an important truth—Jesus was not just raised from the dead, he was raised immortal. What his early followers claimed to see and experience was not some joyous discovery in their own hearts, nor was it a ghost, nor was it a resuscitated corpse.

In the Bible they clearly claim to see, after his death and burial, Jesus of Nazareth, alive, victorious, the risen Lord of life, raised immortal. That is the claim whose truth is to be tested by the jury.

$\mathcal{W}$e understand now exactly what it is we are weighing up.

And there is one unavoidable task that every jury has: you must reach a verdict. The judge doesn't do that, you do that.

You can't sit and listen to the evidence for a few days and then say, "Well, that's all very interesting. I think I'll go home now". No, you are charged with reaching a verdict, and a verdict is unavoidable. The same is true of Jesus: you are charged with reaching a verdict. And you can't escape. An American author wrote a book called *Evidence That Demands a Verdict*. That title also captures the idea I'm trying to explain. Deciding not to decide is deciding against Jesus. At the end of the process your mind will be made up, for good or for ill, forever. And it is forever, because *your* future depends on your verdict.

Part 1

IN COURT

18

The time has come in this case to start examining some of the historical facts. Any lawyer worth his salt (or, better still, worth a large-ish fee) will always start with the facts. It is matters of fact that the jury has to settle.

In the case of Jesus, and what happened to him, we are talking about historical facts—facts that are some 2,000 years old. But historians have developed methods of settling, with a strong balance of probability, even such ancient facts as those.

Some years ago a British lawyer named Val Grieve was invited to the College of Law in Chester to take part in a mock court of inquiry into the resurrection of Jesus from the dead. This 'moot court', as it's called, was organized by the Christian students at the college, who challenged the Humanist students' group to take part in this 'contest of truth' under court-room rules.

As the date drew nearer, Mr Grieve was doing his preparation to take part in the moot court, and he thought it would be a smart move to find out what tack his opponents might take. He made a phone call to find out, and was astonished to discover that the humanists were going to try to argue that the whole of Christianity is a myth. Jesus, they would argue, was a mythical or legendary figure like Robin Hood: someone who never existed.

So, are there any facts, any historical evidences, to show that this claim is false, and the Christian story is well based?

As it happens, members of the jury, there is a pile of solid historical evidence.

Jesus is one of the best-reported, best-evidenced figures of ancient history. There is more historical evidence for Jesus than there is for Julius Caesar—and no one ever suggested that Julius Caesar is a myth! Here are three key facts that history tells us about Jesus:

First, that he is a historical figure who lived some 2,000 years ago.

Second, that he was killed by Roman soldiers by their common method of execution, namely nailing to a wooden cross, and died under the observation of those soldiers.

Third, his dead body was buried in a tomb, and then that tomb was found to be empty. From that moment on the early believers, the first followers, claimed they had seen Jesus and spoken to him after his death and burial.

Three fairly startling facts, I'm sure you'll agree, but not to be dismissed just because they're startling. Three facts to be investigated and examined, not dismissed. And the supporting evidence comes from three sources: from Jewish writers, from pagan writers, and from Christian writers.

To understand these sources you need to think yourself back into the first century world a little.

It was by our standards a primitive world with none of the technological gadgets that we take for granted. You travelled on foot or by horse or camel; ships were driven by the wind, and life was lived at a slower pace. The world of that time around the shores of the Mediterranean Sea was dominated by the power of the Roman Empire. From the great city of Rome conquering armies had gone out, followed by Roman administrators, road builders, and tax collectors. Smaller nations were conquered and dominated by their Roman masters. One of those nations was Judea, the home of the Jewish people.

The local Roman governor in Judea was a man called Pontius Pilate (who plays a key role in the story of Jesus). He had Roman troops under his command stationed in such cities as Jerusalem and Caesarea. The Jewish authorities, for some years, submitted to Roman rule, but there were always those who were rebellious. Finally, in the second half of the first century, a full-scale revolution broke out. For four years, from AD 66 to AD 70, it was fiercely fought, but, eventually, Roman military might crushed the Jewish revolt.

Jesus lived in the early years of the first century, before there was open rebellion. The authorities in Jerusalem were cooperating with their Roman overlords, rather than resisting them. That is the background against which we need to consider the facts recorded by the ancient historians—historical facts about Jesus.

⁓

HOSTILE WITNESSES

Jewish testimony

The most important of the Jewish writers is a man named Flavius Josephus who lived from around AD 37 to around AD 100. He was a soldier and historian, descended from a royal and priestly line. Josephus took an active part in the Jewish revolt against Roman rule starting in AD 66, and was made governor of Galilee. He fought valiantly, but after losing the battle and being captured, he sought, and won, the favour of the Roman general who defeated him—Vespasian (who later became emperor).

Josephus was present with another Roman general, named Titus, at the siege of Jerusalem. When the revolt was crushed he was rewarded with a grant of confiscated land, but spent the rest of his life in Rome. There he wrote three important historical works: his *Autobiography*, his *History of the Jewish Wars* (which is the main historical record of the events of Jewish history in the first century and of the Jewish revolt from AD 66-70); and finally *Antiquities of the Jews*, a history of the Jewish nation from its beginnings up to the period covered by his earlier book.

Josephus was no friend of Christians and no particular admirer of Jesus, but he faithfully recorded the facts that he had. He refers to Jesus twice. Once is a brief reference to James as the brother of Jesus. The second time he says:

> At this time there was a wise man who was called Jesus. And his conduct was good and [he] was known to be virtuous. And many people from among the Jews and other nations became his disciples. Pilate condemned him to be crucified and to die. But those who had become his disciples did not abandon his discipleship. They reported that he had appeared to them three days after his crucifixion and that he was alive...

That's what an ancient historian who is no friend of Christianity writes about Jesus within a lifetime of his death. Is it any wonder that believers are confident that these facts are well grounded in historical reality? There are other references to Jesus in ancient Jewish literature, but this is the most important of them.

Look at all the facts Josephus gives us about Jesus:

> the time in which he lived;
> that he had a brother named James;
> that he was wise and good;

that he had many followers, both Jews and non-Jews;

that governor Pilate condemned him to death;

that his followers reported seeing him alive after his death and burial;

and that those same followers continued to teach others about him.

Pagan testimony

The first of the pagan writers to refer to Jesus was Publius Cornelius Tacitus (AD 55-120), a Roman historian. He was born in the reign of Nero, and lived to be proconsul of Asia under the emperor Trajan—and thus he lived through the reigns of seven of the emperors he describes in his books.

The most important of his writings is called the *Annals*, which records the history of Rome from the death of Augustus (AD 14) to the time of Nero. Tacitus has been described as "a shrewd psychologist who aims to be an exact recorder of events". He has also been called "the greatest historian of ancient Rome".

In the *Annals*, Tacitus records the great fire of Rome of AD 64. The gossip and rumours blamed this fire on the Emperor Nero himself. To shift the blame, Nero accused the Christians of starting the fire. Here is what Tacitus writes:

> To kill the rumours Nero charged and tortured some people hated for their evil practices—the group popularly known as 'Christians'. The founder of this sect, Christ, had been put to death by the governor of Judea, Pontius Pilate, when Tiberius was emperor. Their deadly superstition had been suppressed temporarily, but was beginning to spring up again—not now just in Judea but even in Rome itself...

You can see that Tacitus doesn't really like Christians. If you had been a Christian in Rome at the time, you wouldn't have gone to Tacitus asking for a loan until payday ("Just a few drachmas to tide me over?"). Nevertheless, he provides all this historical information, a parade of historical facts. Such as:

> that Christians were named after their founder, Christ;
> that Christ was put to death by Pontius Pilate;
> that this was during the reign of the emperor Tiberius (AD 14-37);
> that his death suppressed Christianity only for a short while and it broke out again afterwards;
> that it was popular in Judea where it began and had spread as far as Rome.

I realise that after a while the eyes begin to glaze over, but the main thrust is clear: these are historical facts. You can see why Val Grieve wiped the floor with those poor, mislead humanists in that 'moot court'. The facts are solid. Jesus is real. More than that, he is the reality that you must come to terms with.

REAL HISTORY

*L*adies and Gentlemen of the jury, there is more evidence to be considered. There are more historical facts to be weighed in the balance.

More ancient testimony

Somewhat later than both Josephus and Tacitus, but still a useful historical witness, is a bloke named Pliny. Actually, there were two of them, and our concern is with Pliny the Younger (or 'Pliny Junior'). His dad was Pliny the Elder—but you'd worked that out, hadn't you? (By the way, Pliny the Elder died in AD 79 while watching an eruption of Mount Vesuvius—for some reason I keep imagining people saying, "No, don't stand that close, Mr Pliny. Don't stand that... I told him not to stand that close".)

Well, Pliny the Younger was his nephew and adopted son, and he was a noted orator and diligent official under the Emperor Trajan. His frequent letters are factually interesting as they deal with the lives of ordinary, respectable citizens in a provincial town. They also reveal that he was a bit of a crawler, always buttering up the boss and asking his advice on what to do in every situation.

For instance, in AD 112, when he was administrator of the Roman province of Bythinia in north-west Asia Minor, Pliny wrote to his boss Trajan because he was starting to panic about the local Christians. It seems that Christian influence was so strong that the pagan temples had become deserted. A typical public servant who doesn't want to act without orders from the boss, he writes to ask what he should do about this.

Here's how Pliny the Younger describes those early Christians:

They are in the habit of meeting on a certain fixed day before it is light, when they sing…a hymn to Christ as to a god, and bind themselves by a solemn oath not to do any wicked deeds: never to commit any fraud, theft or adultery, never to falsify their word, nor deny a trust when they are called upon to deliver it up. After which it is their custom to separate, and then re-assemble to partake of food—but food of an ordinary and innocent kind.

Now, it's important to understand that this Mr Pliny the Younger (can you imagine having "the" as a middle name?) was no particular friend of Christians. In his letters to Trajan he said that he found Christians to be "unboundedly superstitious" but not "grossly immoral". By the way, he would have called those early Christians "superstitious" because they refused to worship the emperor as a god. But you get the picture—this is an ordinary Roman gentleman of the time who is giving us an accurate, factual picture of early believers.

And in doing so he has told us these five things:

> that they met regularly, once a week (probably on Sundays);
> that they sang hymns;
> that they worshipped Christ as God;
> that they pledged themselves not to do anything wicked;
> and that they lived exemplary moral lives.

You can see why the claim made by humanists, atheists and the rest—about Christianity not being historical—is shot down in flames.

I once had a chap say to me in a tone of absolute certainty: "Oh, well, it's all changed now. What Christians believe now is totally different to what those early Christians believed. It's all been re-written several times." But these very early historical reports, from non-Christian sources (Jewish and pagan sources) prove that this view is totally wrong. Where it came from I can't imagine. Perhaps he read it somewhere, or someone told him. And like a chump he'd just believed it without a scrap of evidence to support it.

After I had talked about these things on the radio once, I received a letter saying: "If Jesus was a real historical figure, why wasn't he ever mentioned by any of the historians of the time?". But of course he was, as we've just seen.

The myths and legends are not peddled by Christians, but by the enemies of Christianity—who tell the most extraordinary stories without a scrap of proof. Sadly, some people seem to believe them just because they're good stories.

Make sure you are not one of them. As a member of the jury, it is the truth that must matter to you—well evidenced, well supported truth, decided on the balance of probabilities, not embraced because it supports a prejudice or confirms a bias.

∾

THE PRIMARY SOURCE

Ladies and Gentlemen of the jury, we have reached the point in this trial where we will consider the Christian witnesses. We have heard from Jewish and pagan historians, and now it's time to hear from the Christians. And this is going to take us (I must warn you) most of the rest of the trial—because there's a bunch of them and they have a lot of information that you need to weigh up when you consider your verdict.

What these witnesses have to say is recorded in the New Testament part of the Bible. And this, fairly obviously, is going to provide us with more information about Jesus than any other source.

So we need to know if this is a reliable source—if we can trust what these New Testament documents tell us.

Perhaps a starting point is to set a time frame, to try to get our chronology right.

It's a pity really that back in the first century they didn't have calendars in the form we have them today. If everyone back in the 0's AD had a little desk calendar, with epigrams at the bottom of each page (things like "All roads lead to Rome—which makes it tough getting to Cairo"), we would be able to nail down precise dates for every event in ancient history, including the events that concern Jesus. But they didn't, so we can't.

We can calculate that Jesus was executed by the Roman authorities (at the request of the local Temple authorities) about a third of the way into the first century. Many historians put the year of his death as AD 33. That gives us a starting point for examining the historical documents.

The very earliest Christian documents are letters, many of them written by a bloke named Paul to early Christian communities. The earliest of those letters dates from no later than AD 50—a mere 17 years after the death of Jesus. That is a short period of time. Any adult can look back over so short a time frame as 17 years and remember the big events that happened quite clearly—and be ready to dispute someone who mis-reports those events.

Here's a list of things those early letters tell us:

> that Jesus was a Jew and a descendant of Abraham and King David;
> that he had a brother named James;
> that he was gentle and humble;
> that his public work was mainly among Jews;
> that he washed the feet of his followers;
> that he was unjustly and cruelly treated by the authorities;
> that he was put on trial before the local Roman governor, Pontius Pilate;
> that he was executed;
> that he came back from the dead, and was seen by many of his early followers, sometimes alone and sometimes in groups
> —and many other things besides.

Clearly the Christian story is not a later invention—it comes from the very time of Jesus and his contemporaries. Whether you agree or disagree with the story, you must admit that it *is* the real story that the real early followers of Jesus told, and appeared to believe themselves.

At the beginning of the New Testament part of the Bible are four short biographies of Jesus, named after the chaps who wrote them: Matthew, Mark, Luke and John. These four documents are called the 'gospels' (the word just means 'good news'). Are they early documents or later inventions?

One distinguished scholar, Dr J. A. T. Robinson, points out that none of them make any reference to the great Jewish

Roman war of AD 66-70, and so all of them must have been written before AD 66. In other words, the evidence we have available to examine, Ladies and Gentlemen of the jury, is the authentic early evidence.

This is the real story about Jesus, as told and believed within just a few years (half a lifetime) of his death. Through these documents we can authentically reach back and touch the past. The next part of the task is to form some judgement of that past.

~

RELIABILITY OF RECORDS

We have established, Ladies and Gentlemen of the Jury, that our records of these eye-witness accounts are reliable. But what of the witnesses themselves? Are they likely to be trustworthy?

Some people are going to say something like: "but we can't accept this evidence of the early believers; they are biased; their belief is their bias; their evidence is tainted by what they believe about Jesus". But this is not a sound objection. It's like refusing to accept the evidence of an eyewitness to a road accident just because he was an eyewitness and has a firm opinion about what he saw. We accept the evidence of such a person. Of course, we accept it critically: we examine it and study it and think about it. But we don't reject it out of hand. To do so would be to ban all eyewitnesses from our courts of law.

Some other people might object that, even if the eyewitness accounts were genuinely from the time of Jesus or shortly after, and even if the witnesses were reliable, we can't be sure that our modern New Testaments are the same as the original documents. Surely they could have been added to, or changed, sometime during the last 2,000 years?

It's a fair question. If, as a journalist, I was researching a story about an event that happened 20 or 30 or 40 years ago, one of the places I would start would be with newspaper files. I would go to a central library where they have newspapers filed on microfilm and read the papers for the dates in question. But, hang about, they didn't have newspapers back in Jesus' day! Come to think of it, they didn't even have printing! Back in those days documents (like the New Testament documents) were circulated by being copied out *by hand*. And, we all know that when we copy things by hand we make mistakes (well, not you, you're clever—but me, I make mistakes).

So how can we be sure that lots of errors or changes or 'fictionalization' or something of the sort, didn't creep in as these documents circulated in hand-written copies? The answer is that this same problem applies to the whole of ancient history—right up to the invention of printing in the 15th century.

So, how do historians usually test the reliability of hand-written copies of documents if they're researching, say, the Roman Emperors or Egyptian Pharaohs?

We don't have the original documents (these are called the 'autographs'—Julius Caesar's own account of the *Gallic Wars* in his own handwriting, or in the handwriting of the slave he was dictating to, for instance). Since we don't have these, the historians are interested in how early is the *earliest* copy. That is, how close to the events, how close to the time of composition, is the earliest copy we have? In the case of Caesar's *Gallic Wars*, the oldest copy in existence comes from some 900 years after it was first written, 900 years after the events it records.

And this is fairly typical for most ancient historical documents.

Except the New Testament, which is about 1000% better in this respect.

There is a collection of ancient documents called the Chester Beatty Papyri (so called because the words are written on papyrus—a primitive form of paper made from the pith of water plants). These Chester Beatty Papyri contain most of the New Testament and date not from 900 years later, but from less than 200 years later. Then there's something called the Bodmer Papyrus containing most of John's Gospel and dating to a time span of perhaps 70 years after John's Gospel was composed. In the British city of Manchester, in the John Rylands Library, there is a fragment of John's Gospel that dates to, perhaps, some 40 years after it was first written. And there's a controversial German scholar who claims that one particular fragment is a small part of Matthew's Gospel and dates to the middle of the first century.

The oldest copies of the New Testament are closer in date to the events they record than any other documents from ancient history.

The other thing is, we have lots and lots of these copies. With most ancient documents you're lucky if there's still ten of them surviving. In the case of the New Testament, there are more than 2,000 ancient copies.

To write off the New Testament would be to write off *the whole* of ancient history.

We have the witnesses, we can hear their voices—better than any other ancient voices. That being so, we had better take seriously their claim to be eyewitnesses to Jesus.

THE COUNTER-ARGUMENT

I still feel some scepticism in the air. Perhaps some television show has recently claimed that the New Testament documents are not real, historical, eyewitness records. What are we to make then, members of the jury, of these documents in the Bible that claim to provide eyewitness information about Jesus?

Well, here's the basic legal rule. The great British lawyer Sir Norman Anderson said that an "account should be accepted as *prima facie* reliable unless there is evidence to show that the opposite is the case". In other words, we don't ask these documents to prove themselves—we accept them *unless* there are arguments proving we shouldn't. That's the basic and proper legal procedure.

If I may digress for a moment, the best way to make this clear is to tell you about an organization called "The Jesus Seminar", because they don't do it.

They are people who don't believe in Jesus. Indeed, they don't believe in the God of the Bible. Their stated objective is to change the content and nature of the historic Christian faith.

(This would be like a bunch of wealthy capitalists calling themselves "The Karl Marx Seminary", or a bunch of Communists establishing "The Free Market Seminar".)

"The Jesus Seminar" consists of 75 people who meet twice a year to make pronouncements about the authenticity of the words and deeds of Jesus. The group comprises liberal Catholics, Protestants, Jews and atheists. Most are men and most are professors, although their number includes one pastor, one film-maker and three women.

Their purpose is to change the way people think about Jesus, and to this end they are very keen on publicity. They write books and articles, issue press releases, have held a TV summit, give interviews to the media, distribute tapes, and there is even talk of a movie based on their work. "The Jesus Seminar" is a radical fringe of New Testament scholarship, and there is no reason to take them seriously.

Often their scholarship consists of quoting one another in their books and articles, and their conclusions are based on their assumptions, not the evidence. The unexamined assumption that is the foundation of "The Jesus Seminar" can be labelled "anti-supernaturalism". That is, they start by assuming that God is either not interested in this world, or is powerless to act in this world, or simply doesn't exist at all.

When you start with that as your assumption—your presupposition, your bias—you will, of course, have to deny all the miracles. But the biographies of Jesus in the New Testament part of the Bible are full of miracles. How do these people cope with that? They do it by claiming that these biographies, or Gospels, are fictional works written long after the time of Jesus. The problem—for them, not us—is that there is good evidence for dating those Gospels as being early, eyewitness documents.

The scholar J. A. T. Robinson, whom I referred to earlier, has written about this in the sort of language scholars understand. His conclusion was that the Gospels were written between AD 40 and AD 60. That is, between seven and 27 years after the death of Jesus at the hands of Roman soldiers.

But even if the Gospels were written a little later than that, there is still not enough time for myths and legends to develop.

Scholars have studied how long it takes for myths and legends to be added to a true, historical story about a person, and it takes hundreds of years. Even "The Jesus Seminar" people themselves don't date the Gospels late enough to have allowed time for that sort of thing to have happened.

Here's a useful comparison: the first biographies of Alexander the Great were written 400 years after his death, and yet historians regard them as generally trustworthy. In other words, for around 500 years after his death the story of Alexander the Great was kept more or less intact: the legends and myths emerged over the *next* 500 years. In the case of Jesus, it's clearly not going to make much difference whether a particular Gospel was written 25 years after his death or 55: it's still not enough time for legends and myths to take over.

And "The Jesus Seminar" has no answer for those arguments, except to say that they don't fit in with their prejudices.

It's as if you found yourself on a criminal jury, and when you retired to the jury room one your fellow jurors (the goose in the group—there's a goose in every group) announced that he had decided the accused was guilty the minute he saw him. "And then", he explains, "I had to consider all the evidence in the light of the decision I had already made that the man was guilty. So I've had to dismiss as unreliable anything that suggests his inno-cence, and consider only the testimony that supports his guilt".

What would you say to such a juror?

Wouldn't you say: "Hang on, we were supposed to make our minds on the *basis* of the evidence, not make up our minds first and then filter the evidence". I think you'd say something very much like that. Because you are smart enough to see what's wrong with such an attitude. There, then, is the basic legal rule. Sir Norman Anderson said it well, when he said that an "account should be accepted as *prima facie* reliable unless there is evidence to show that the opposite is the case".

And there is no such evidence to suggest the accounts are unreliable. When you look at the actual evidence, as opposed to blind prejudice, you can see why the distinguished historian Sir Frederick Kenyon, came to this conclusion:

> It cannot be too strongly asserted that in substance the text of the Bible is certain. Especially is this the case with the New Testament. The number of manuscripts of the New Testament, of early translations from it, and of quo-tations from it in the oldest writers of the Church, is so large that it is practically certain that the true reading of every doubtful passage is preserved in one or other of these ancient authorities. This can be said of no other ancient book in the world.

EXHIBIT ONE

And now, members of the jury, here is the first piece of evidence to be placed before you. If we could label this 'Exhibit One' for the respondent, please your honour? Thank you. It is, as you can see, an empty tomb. (It's a good thing we're not in a real court—an empty tomb, large and made of rock, would be a heavy item for a lawyer's clerk to lug around!)

To understand the tomb, we need to be clear about the 'common ground' or 'agreed facts'.

In the light of the evidence from contemporary and near contemporary historians, it is agreed that:

> Jesus was a real historical person, a Jew, who lived in the Roman province of Judea in the first third of the first century. He was condemned to death and executed under the orders of the Roman procurator (that just means 'governor') of the province, Pontius Pilate, probably in AD 33. After his execution his tomb was found empty.

The rest of the information comes from the Christian historians. They tell us that Jesus was arrested at night, on the outskirts of the city of Jerusalem, well away from the crowds. The Temple authorities who organized his arrest were afraid of his popular following, and so arranged for the arrest to made 'on the quiet' as it were. His trial was rushed through overnight and in the early hours of the morning.

At first light he was taken to the Fortress Antonia, the Roman barracks in Jerusalem, where Pontius Pilate was temporarily in residence. (His permanent residence was on the coast, in the city of Caesarea.) With some reluctance, Pilate agreed to pronounce the death sentence.

A Roman military execution squad led Jesus, and two other prisoners, to a hill called 'Golgotha', just outside the walls of the city. There he was nailed to a wooden cross with six-inch iron spikes through his feet and wrists. He hung on the cross for some hours, and then died.

One of his followers, who was a wealthy man, asked permission to take charge of the body. After checking with the soldiers on duty at the execution that Jesus was really dead, Pilate released the body to Joseph of Arimathea. With the assistance of another man, named Nicodemus, he prepared the body for burial, by wrapping it in a shroud with the usual embalming perfumes used in those days, and buried it in a rock tomb that he had purchased for his own use. This was, in effect, a small artificial cave dug straight into the solid rock of a cliff. When the body was laid inside, the entrance was sealed by rolling a large rock across the opening. Some of the women who had been with Jesus followed Joseph and Nicodemus and saw where the tomb was in which Jesus was buried.

The following day the Temple authorities asked Governor Pilate to place an armed guard on the tomb site, and this he did.

By the early hours of the next morning the tomb was empty.

The rock sealing the entrance had been rolled back, and the tomb was clearly vacant. Panicked by this, the Temple authorities bribed the soldiers on guard duty to say, "His disciples came during the night and stole him away while we were asleep" (Matthew 28:13). That was never a very convincing lie: if they were asleep, how could they know what happened? But the very fact that they were asked to lie establishes that there was something that needed explaining: namely, an empty tomb.

THEORIES

It was the women who found the tomb empty, early on that Sunday morning after the crucifixion. They were there because they assumed that the body of Jesus had not been properly prepared for burial—that it had not been properly embalmed. Well, it was two men who did the burying, and what would men know about laying out a corpse? That was something women were specialists in.

When they arrived in the garden, at the tomb where they had seen Jesus laid to rest, they found the stone rolled away and the tomb empty. They had some difficulty persuading the others, the men in the group, that this was really the case. But when the men, lead by John and Peter, went and saw for themselves, they were convinced.

When you look at the clear beliefs of the early believers, as recorded by the Jewish and pagan historians, and when you look at the stir that the story of Jesus created, and how quickly it spread throughout the Roman Empire, there can be little doubt that the tomb was really empty. A Jewish scholar, Geza Vermes, reached this conclusion:

> In the end, when every argument has been considered and weighed, the only conclusion acceptable to the historian must be…that the women who set out to pay their last respects to Jesus found to their consternation, not a body, but an empty tomb.

But the problem with an object like an empty tomb is that it is just a silent object. It doesn't tell us quite enough in itself.

What matters is how it came to be empty. And that is the key issue here. So, how can we account for the tomb being empty? There are perhaps half a dozen possible explanations, and we'll work through them one at a time.

The first has to be fraud. This is the story that the soldiers on guard at the tomb were bribed to spread: "His disciples came during the night and stole him away while we were asleep" (Matthew 28:13). Does this explanation hold water? I've already pointed out that the story the guards told was illogical, but, nevertheless, might it be true that the followers of Jesus stole his body?

In the first place, whatever actually happened to the guards, there were certainly some guards on duty at the tomb. Were they Jewish Temple Guards or Roman soldiers? The records don't make this clear, and historians have disagreed about it over the years. In either case it's unlikely they would have allowed the body to be stolen. If the guards were the Jewish, they would have been punished for allowing the theft of the body. If you were a Temple Guard you were forbidden to sit down or even lean against anything while on guard duty (and you think your job's tough!). But it gets worse: a member of the Temple Guard who fell asleep while on guard duty was beaten and burned with his own clothes.

However, I am inclined to think that it wasn't Jewish guards, but Roman soldiers on duty at the tomb. When I was researching my detective novel on this subject (*The Case of the Vanishing Corpse*), I telephoned leading historian Dr Paul Barnett to ask his opinion. Paul said it could have been either, but he was inclined, as were most historians, to lean towards the Roman soldier option. This being so, there would have been four soldiers on guard duty at the tomb. (In *The Case of the Vanishing Corpse* I reduced this to two to make it easier to handle the characters, but a standard Roman guard was a patrol of four soldiers.)

They too were part of a tough, disciplined force, and would have been severely punished if they had really fallen asleep while on guard duty. In any case, one or two might have fallen asleep, but not all four.

So, first, for the disciples to have stolen the body they would have had to deal with four tough, battle-hardened Roman soldiers. A bunch of fishermen would hardly have been a match for trained soldiers.

Second, if they stole the body, why weren't they charged with theft? Under Roman law the corpse of someone executed by the authorities was the property of the state. But the disciples were never charged.

Third, they were not psychologically capable of stealing a corpse. Anyone who thinks they were has never grieved over the death of a loved one. These people had just seen someone they loved and admired deeply die a horrible death. They were in shock, in mourning. Heartbroken people don't concoct and carry out grave robbing plots within 36 hours of suffering such a shocking loss. They were depressed, disheartened, dispirited and leaderless—in no fit state to do anything of the sort.

Fourth, what motive would they have had for doing this? The body was safe in a rock tomb, and they could have turned that garden tomb into a shrine to the memory of Jesus: why steal the body?

Fifth, if there really was a conspiracy to steal the body and pretend that Jesus had come back from the dead, they would never have got away with it. Sooner or later one of the conspirators would have cracked and told the truth—particularly bearing in mind that they all suffered for their faith and most died a martyr's death.

Finally, if fraud is the way to account for the empty tomb

then those first followers were not just deceived, but deliberate deceivers. The whole movement was based on a lie. And this is totally out of keeping with what we know about their characters. And again, a con man won't die for his lie, and these men died for their faith. Fraud does not explain the empty tomb. So, the empty tomb is still there—a hard piece of evidence demanding an explanation.

❧

EXPLAINING THE GRAVE

*M*embers of the jury, we are in the process of trying to account for this vital and central piece of evidence—the empty tomb you see before you. (Well, no, you don't actually see it before you, but use your imagination.) We've ruled out fraud on the part of the disciples.

The next theory that has been offered to explain the empty tomb without Jesus actually coming back from the dead in some powerful, supernatural way, is something called the 'swoon and revival' theory. This is the notion that Jesus did not actually die on the cross, he simply fainted, or 'swooned' (to use an old fashioned word), and later in the nice, cool tomb he revived, pushed away the stone sealing the entrance and escaped.

This is not a new theory, it's been around a long time. Over 600 years after the death of Jesus, an Islamic sect called the

Ahmadiya came up with this story that Jesus escaped from his tomb, after which he met his disciples in Galilee, and then walked to North India, where he died at the age of 120.

This theory has long been a favourite of unbelievers. It is, for instance, the idea behind a book called *The Passover Plot*, with the additional twist that it's there claimed that Jesus always intended to fake his own death.

A variation on this 'swoon and revival' notion is advanced by Barbara Theiring in her highly publicized books.

By the way, Barbara Theiring is one of those people who claim the New Testament does not actually say what it appears to say. She's one of those who claim to have found a secret code hidden in the text which she, and she alone, has decoded. The interesting thing about these people is that when they supposedly 'crack the code' they all find a different message. So Barbara Theiring is one of those whose 'decoding' doesn't agree with anyone else's 'decoding', and who has failed to persuade the community of scholars to agree with her.

Even so, we need to look at this 'swoon and revival' theory seriously.

Could it account for the empty tomb? Well, it runs into a number of obstacles.

In the first place, the people doing the crucifying were Roman soldiers who were experts in what they did. They did lots of crucifixions and they didn't get them wrong. It was a common form of execution in the Roman Empire—on one occasion, during a mass rebellion, 6,000 people were crucified in one day. These were professional executioners, and it's unlikely they would have made the basic mistake of pronouncing a man dead if he wasn't.

Second, in the Roman army it paid to be very careful. It was a tough, disciplined army. For example, if a Roman soldier was guarding a prisoner, and that prisoner escaped, the soldier was required to serve the rest of the prisoner's sentence. That's one tough army! That's a system you don't mess with. In that sort of army you can be certain the execution squad made doubly and triply sure they had made no mistakes. Those they said were dead, were really dead.

Third, when the governor, Pontius Pilate, was approached and asked to release the body of Jesus, he was surprised to hear that Jesus was already dead. And Jesus really did die quite quickly for a victim of crucifixion: in just hours, and some of them hung on for days. So the governor sent a messenger to his soldiers to ask if it was true that Jesus was already dead. If they hadn't checked before, they would most certainly have checked very carefully the minute the boss's message arrived. A Roman governor was a boss you didn't muck around with. These are all good reasons for rejecting the 'swoon and revival' theory.

Fourth, there is another important detail that makes this clear. We are told that when the soldiers were making sure Jesus was dead they thrust a spear into his side "bringing a sudden flow of blood and water" (John 19:34). This is the kind of detail that assures us we are reading an eyewitness account at this point. The distinguished doctor, Professor A. Rendle Short, Professor of Surgery at Bristol University, said that this flow of blood and water means that the spear pierced the stomach, from which watery fluid flowed, and the heart and other major organs of the upper chest (where the blood came from, of course—at this point Jesus had not been dead long enough for all the blood to have coagulated). "Needless to say", explains the professor, "such a wound would be instantly fatal if the victim was not already dead, which indeed he was".

Fifth, the 'swoon and revival' theory fails to take into account how crucifixion kills its victims. They basically asphyxiate. When they are first put on the cross they support their weight with their hands and feet (no matter how painful this is), but as time wears on, and as the pain increases and physical exhaustion sets in, they can no longer support their own weight. They sag forward, and are unable to expand their lungs to breathe—hence they suffocate to death.

If they are slow in dying and the soldiers want to hurry them up, what they do is break their legs. This means that there is no way they can support their own weight, and they asphyxiate quickly. That happened on the occasion when Jesus was cruci-fied. Wanting to hurry up proceedings the soldiers broke the legs of the two men who were crucified alongside Jesus; but when they came to Jesus himself they found that he was already dead and they didn't need to break his legs. Yet another detail that reassures us we are looking at an eyewitness report here, and yet another detail that tells us that Jesus was definitely and certainly dead—pronounced to be so by those experts in death, a Roman military execution squad.

Sixth, if this whole fanciful notion were true, if Jesus had only fainted on the cross (and I'm just saying 'if' here) he could never have escaped from the tomb. The rock that sealed the entrance to the tomb was heavy and awkward to move. A desperately injured, weakened man, alone, from inside the tomb, could never have moved it. So this so-called 'swoon and revival' theory certainly can't explain an empty tomb, because the tomb would not have been empty—Jesus would have been trapped inside.

And finally, there is no way this weak, beaten, battered,

exhausted man could have persuaded his followers that he was the triumphant conqueror of death. You know what it's like when someone has just survived a dangerous, harrowing, exhausting experience—everything about them conveys the idea that they have just had a narrow escape. But that was not the impression those first followers had of the risen Jesus: they saw him not as a survivor of a narrow escape, but as a triumphant conqueror, as the risen Lord, as the Prince of Life. A sick, fainting, exhausted man could not convey that impression.

There you have seven different reasons for saying the 'swoon and revival' theory is a dud. Their collective weight is overwhelming and decisive. So, the empty tomb remains empty—and unexplained. It remains a powerful piece of evidence pointing us towards the strange truth about who Jesus was and what really happened to him.

❧

ALTERNATIVE
EXPLANATIONS

We are in the process of trying to understand the item currently before us on the exhibits table of the court, members of the jury—namely one empty tomb. How did it come to be empty, and what does it tell us about Jesus?

We've examined and disposed of the fraud and swoon theories for explaining the emptiness of the tomb, so that daunting emptiness remains before us as a challenge. Here are a few brief explanations that have been tried on over the years—none of these work, I must say, but let's look at them and see why.

First, there's the idea that when the women went looking for the tomb on the Sunday morning it was early, the dawn light was dim (it might have been misty) and they simply went to the wrong tomb. They found a new tomb, not yet occupied, standing open, and mistook it for the one in which Jesus had been buried.

The problem with that explanation is that such a mistake would have been quickly corrected. One of the other disciples would have said, "Hang about, are you sure you've got the right place?". Or the Temple authorities would have directed people to the correct tomb—after all they were instrumental in having a guard placed on the correct tomb, so they knew which one it was. They could have pointed to the correct tomb, with its entrance still closed and sealed with a large rock. They could have rolled back the rock and shown the dead body inside. They did none of these things because they couldn't—this mistake was never made. The tomb in question was always the right one.

Second, someone once suggested that the Temple authorities, who had ordered the death of Jesus, might have taken his body from the tomb in order to prevent it becoming a martyr's shrine. After all, as I said, they had organized the guard, so they, of all people, could order the guards to "look the other way". Problem: the Temple authorities were deeply embarrassed and angry about the claims made by those first followers, that Jesus had come back from the dead. If they had the body they would have produced it to refute the claim. Christianity could have been stopped cold, stopped dead, in the few first days, simply by hanging the carcass of the dead Jesus from the gates of Jerusalem. The Temple authorities didn't do this, because they couldn't—proof that they did not take the body out of the tomb.

Something similar has been suggested with respect to the Roman authorities. After all, legally the body was their property, so they could have removed it if they wished. The problem is: why would they wish to? They had no reason to remove the body from the tomb. And then again, even if they had, they were in league with the Temple authorities, and they undoubtedly would have produced the body as soon as the resurrection story started to spread. They didn't because they couldn't—they did not empty the tomb of its contents. So, we're still faced with the issue of this unexplained empty tomb.

One final suggestion has been made to try to avoid the obvious significance of this evidence. And that is that grave robbers took the body.

The suggestion is that among the visitors to Jerusalem for the big Passover Festival (that was on at the time) were some professional grave robbers who saw the crucifixion, and saw the sign that governor Pilate had nailed to the cross on which Jesus hung, saying 'King of the Jews' in three languages (Latin, Greek and Hebrew). Such signs were attached to crosses to identify the dying man's crime or crimes. Governor Pilate's sign was accusing Jesus of the crime of claiming political power (which, of course, he never did—his trial had been a mockery, a parade of lies and injustice).

In those days, kings were often buried with their treasure. So, this conspiracy theory goes, the grave robbers could have spied on the burial of Jesus and later returned to rob the grave of the treasure they expect it to contain.

However, this theory also doesn't hold water. First, if, upon entering the tomb, these men found no treasure, why on earth would they then take the body—which was of no value? There is no reason for such behaviour. Second, the tomb *did* contain something of value: a large amount (a very large amount— almost 30 kilos by my calculations) of the expensive ointments and perfumes used in embalming in those days, or buried with the corpse if there was no time to do the actual embalming—a mixture of myrrh and aloes. Now, all the earliest records agree on this point: the body was gone but the linen cloths in which the ointments were wrapped were left behind.

What sort of thieves steal a valueless body, but leave behind an expensive and valuable amount of myrrh and aloes (worth, as far as I can find out, hundreds of drachma)? Thieves don't do that sort of thing! Thieves steal items of value, not items of no value. This explanation, too, turns out to be something that fails the 'balance of probabilities' test—and we have run out of ways to explain the empty tomb. Well, almost.

THE 'EMBARRASSING' EXPLANATION

*M*embers of the jury, the tomb in which Jesus was buried was found to be empty a mere 36 hours after his death and burial. We have examined every suggested natural explanation for that fact—and all have failed. Is it so very unreasonable to say that if natural explanations fail, we should turn to supernatural ones?

Sir Arthur Conan Doyle put these words into the mouth of his famous character Sherlock Holmes: "When you have eliminated the impossible, whatever remains, however improbable, must be the truth".

We quite often feel uncomfortable with supernatural explanations these days—I suspect because there is a bad odor that hangs around that word 'supernatural'. We associate it with B-grade horror movies from Hollywood and silly ghost stories, and, since it is reasonable to dismiss such things as nonsense, we dismiss the whole 'supernatural'—and everything it represents—as being just plain silly.

But, members of the jury, we must dismiss all our prejudices, all our biases, and all emotion, and look coolly and rationally at the possibilities. The only way to dismiss the supernatural as totally ridiculous is if you believe that the material realm, the physical realm, is all there is; if you believe that there is matter and energy, in a physical sense, and nothing else.

Most people, I put it to you members of the jury, don't accept such a narrow materialism as a total account of what exists. Most people take the common sense view that such things as consciousness, intentions, thoughts, ideas and so on are not physical, not material. These things, and much more besides, constitute a non-material, non-physical realm of existence.

It is not so very strange to postulate a further realm, a 'super'-natural one.

But who or what is there in the supernatural realm powerful enough to have an enormous impact on the physical, natural realm; to bring someone back from the dead, to empty a tomb that had contained a dead man? The answer is obvious.

That other realm—'supernature'—is the realm in which is found the Consciousness that planned the Universe, the Mind behind it all, the Intelligent Designer, the Creator God— the Big Brain Behind the Big Bang. Such a Being most certainly has the power to create planets. Therefore, such a Being most certainly has the power to bring Jesus back to life, back out of the tomb in which he was buried, if he so chose.

Here's what the Bible says about the greatness and power of God:

> Lift your eyes and look to the heavens: Who created all these?...Do you not know? Have you not heard? The LORD is the everlasting God, the Creator of the ends of the earth. He will not grow tired or weary, and his under-standing no one can fathom (Isaiah 40:26, 28).

This—the power of God—is the *only* reasonable explanation for the empty tomb.

❧

WITNESSES

*M*embers of the jury, what we have done so far is to examine the evidence of the empty tomb. But, as someone once pointed out, an empty tomb is just an empty tomb: not a living Jesus.

So, we need to look beyond the empty tomb at further evidence, and further testimony. At this point we are going to begin examining witnesses who claimed to see Jesus alive, and speak with him, after his death, after his execution at the hands of the Roman death squad. They claim they saw and met with Jesus after he was dead and buried, and that the Jesus they met with was the same Jesus they had known before his death, and that he was not dead when they saw him, or even recovering from near death, but powerfully and triumphantly alive.

We can call the events these witnesses give their testimony about, the 'appearances' of the risen Jesus.

At the end of each of the four short biographies of Jesus, the four 'gospels' (Matthew, Mark, Luke and John) are accounts of visits to the grave of Jesus (which was found to be empty) and of Jesus appearing alive to his friends.

But let me first pre-empt some of your objections to these witnesses who will claim they saw Jesus alive after his execution.

Some will try to explain away their testimony by saying, "Sure these people are sincere. And they sincerely believe what they're saying. But they are sincerely wrong: deluded, deceived. They are the victims or either wish-fulfillment or hallucinations". Those are real possibilities, so we need to examine them.

Referring to the testimony given by Mary Magdalene, one unbeliever writes: "The passion of an hallucinated woman gives the world a resurrected God". Is it as simple as that? What, in fact, is an hallucination? The American Psychiatric Association's official definition says an hallucination is "a false sensory perception in the absence of an actual, sensory stimulus".

So, when the alcoholic in the grip of *delirium tremens* thinks he sees huge, black insects crawling out of cracks in the walls, when there are (in reality) no such things in the room with him—that is an hallucination. Did something similar happen to those first followers of Jesus? There are a number of problems with that proposal.

First, hallucinations are private and individual experiences. They are caused by a chemical or electrical imbalance inside a brain—and such an imbalance happens in one brain at a time. If you were in the room with the alcoholic having an attack of *delirium tremens* and he was screaming and pointing at the hoard of huge, black insects approaching him, you would not see the insects. The imbalance, the disturbance, is only in his brain and it doesn't affect yours. He hallucinates, you don't. In the case of the postmortem appearances of Jesus, he sometimes appeared to individuals, but more often to groups. Individually he appeared to Mary Magdalene, Peter, James and Paul. But he also appeared to a group of women, to two travellers walking to the town of Emmaus, to a group of ten men in an upper room, a week later to a group of eleven, to a group of them on the shores of Lake Galilee, and, on one occasion, he appeared to 500 people at once. It is very difficult to assert that those sorts of group appearances can be accounted for by hallucination.

Second, not only are they a personal, individualistic thing, but hallucinations happen to certain types of people who are vulnerable to them for particular reasons. That vulnerability might be caused by chemical abuse (alcohol or drugs) or, perhaps, by a certain personality type—highly imaginative, highly sensitive. But Jesus appeared, postmortem, to many different types of people—men and women, fishermen and intellectuals. They can't all be written off as 'vulnerable personality types'.

Third, hallucinations are usually restricted to particular types of places. A place with dim lighting and a suggestive atmosphere may well provide favourable circumstances for an hallucination. Jesus appeared, postmortem, in all kinds of places: in a garden in the morning, in a dining room at night, beside a road in blazing sunlight, beside a lake, on a hillside: hardly a collection of suitably 'spooky' places to trigger hallucinations.

And fourth, hallucinations usually increase in intensity and occur regularly over a long period. They become worse (not better), perhaps obsessional, and sometimes lead to insanity. However, those first followers of Jesus stopped seeing him exactly 40 days after his death and burial. That is uncharacteristic of hallucinations. In fact, all of this is highly uncharacteristic of hallucinations.

So, it is reasonable to conclude, on the balance of probabilities, that however we account for these postmortem appearances of Jesus, hallucinations are ruled out.

Well, if not hallucinations, then might all of this have been an example of wish-fulfilment?

Imagine, for instance, the case of a mum whose teenage daughter has run away from home. The distraught mum might quite often imagine she sees her missing daughter—in a crowd, across the street, or passing in a bus—because she desperately wants to see her daughter. The 'appearances' of her daughter are the product of her own wishes, they are 'wish-fulfilment' appearances. Could that have been the case with the first followers of Jesus?

For it to be the case, there are certain conditions that would have to be met. For example, those people who claimed to see Jesus, postmortem, would first have to have deeply wanted to see him, and second believed it would be possible to see him, and third expected to see him, and fourth, have immediately and joyfully identified him as the one they wanted to see. The very earliest written records don't really show those conditions being met.

First, there is no sign that the first followers wished Jesus to come back. They were mainly depressed, disheartened, dispirited and ready to give up. They were also fearful: the boss had been killed and the authorities might come after them next. Because of their fear they had scattered—on the day of the execution many of them had fled to the nearby town of Bethany. There is no evidence of wishing or wanting in that behaviour.

Second, there is no evidence that they thought it possible for Jesus to come back from the dead. They had seen him raise others from the dead, but they behaved as if his power had died with him. They talked about returning to their old trades (for many, that was fishing): there is no thought here that it's possible they soon may see Jesus again.

Third, they most certainly had no expectation that he would return to life. Jesus had clearly taught them that he must be put to death, and then conquer death, and come back from the dead, but (like so many of his other teachings) this didn't 'gel' with them until it had actually happened. Mary Magdalene saw a man in the garden near the tomb and assumed it was the gardener. It turned out to be Jesus. Two travellers walking to the town of Emmaus were joined by a third—they assumed he was a stranger. He turned out to be Jesus. It's not the case that Mary saw a gardener and thought he was Jesus: she saw Jesus and thought he was the gardener. It's not the case that the travellers saw a stranger and thought he was Jesus: they saw Jesus and thought he was a stranger. There's no evidence here of expectation of seeing Jesus—in fact, the very opposite.

And finally, far from joyfully welcoming the risen Jesus, those early disciples took several moments to realise who it was, and had to be convinced their eyes didn't deceive them, and that it was really who it appeared to be.

Thomas is the classic case of this. When the others said they had seen Jesus he refused to accept their word for it. He insisted that he would have to touch the wounds Jesus received when being crucified before he'd swallow that story. When he did see the risen, living Jesus, he was simply bowled over by the power of his presence and believed. But his first inclination had been to doubt, and doubt deeply. What was true for Thomas to a greater extent is true for all the disciples to a lesser extent— there was a definite slowness and reluctance to believe the evidence of their own senses.

It was only when the evidence was overwhelming that they admitted that Jesus was, indeed, back from the dead. Their reaction was, in fact, in terms of human psychology, entirely normal. So don't be put off if you find it hard to believe. You must be prepared to do what those first followers did: having examined the evidence, and the testimony, you must be open to accept the facts as the facts—however remarkable they strike you as being.

OVERCOMING PREJUDICE

*L*et me remind you that the charge that is given to all jurors when they are sworn in for jury service, is to leave behind all prejudice, bias, and emotion, and to judge the case simply on the facts. But that is a hard thing to do.

Our biases and prejudices are deeply built into us. If the accused in a criminal trial has a face, or a manner, that we take an instant dislike to, it is going to be difficult to be dispassionate in our judgement. But that difficulty is exactly the task we must undertake if we are ever to get at the truth.

We run into this problem very sharply when we look at who Jesus was and what really happened to him—especially the claim that he came back from the dead.

We have, in our modern world, a built-in bias against miracles, against the supernatural. We are reluctant to accept such stories. We look with frank scepticism at ghost stories, and we think all those people who believe they've been abducted by aliens are just a bit dotty.

The comical thing about this resistance to the supernatural is that the vast majority of people believe in God—or claim to believe in God—when they fill in their census forms. That puts most people in the rather odd position of thinking that God is there, and that he is basically unemployed.

What do they imagine God does to achieve his goals? Do they think God mutters to himself, "Dear Me, I mustn't interfere with the regular running of things, that would look like a miracle, and the poor dears can't cope with miracles". Is that how they imagine God's mind works? There is God, sitting on his hands (figuratively speaking) doing nothing, holding in check that astonishing power that created planets and whole galaxies, because... well, why? Because we don't want to believe that the God who is there takes a hand in things sometimes? Because we are a bit frightened by the whole prospect of an interventionist God?

On the basis of absolutely nothing but blind prejudice, millions of otherwise intelligent people will insist that God would not intervene in human affairs or the regular running of the natural world. Why are they so insistent? Because they have some special insight into the mind of God? Or because the last thing they ever want to contemplate is the terrifying idea of an interventionist God? When my friend Terry said to me, "God wouldn't bother with this small, unimportant planet", he had no reason and no evidence to support his confident claim.

In fact, his confidence and firm insistence seemed to be designed to make up for the lack of evidence. How could Terry possibly know that? Had he asked God? Had he been given special supernatural insight into the mind of God? No, he had, he insisted, "just figured it out for himself". But, I went on, you must have "figured it out" on some basis. Terry thought for a moment, and then said, "Well, look, if I was God, with an entire universe, I wouldn't take any interest in small, insect-like creatures like us, crawling around on the surface of an insignificant planet". I, of course, fell about laughing. Terry had told me a lot about himself—and nothing at all about God.

The whole trouble we have with miracles springs from our habit, and a bad habit at that, of making guesses about God based on projecting our own egos onto the cosmic scale. God has capacities vastly beyond our imaginations.

He not only has the capacity to make and manage the universe, he has capacities of care, and love, and interest that we cannot even begin to imagine. This being so, you cannot rule out the possibility of miracles.

If there is a God—a personal, powerful Creator God—as most people believe, then miracles have got to be on the list of things that might happen, or might have happened, at special moments, for special reasons. If there is even the *possibility* of God, then there is the *possibility* of miracles. Including the possibility of this particular, significant miracle: Jesus coming back from the dead.

❧

WITNESS:
MARY MAGDALENE

It's now time for us to start calling witnesses. Let's begin with the evidence of Mary Magdalene. We might picture her entering the witness stand, taking the oath, and then stating her name in a firm, clear voice. But perhaps at this point it would be better for us to stop picturing what her manner might be like, and, instead, consult her real evidence as we have it before us, because we have the evidence of Mary Magdalene reported for us in those biographies of Jesus I have already referred to. We can consult her evidence "on paper" as it were. And that is what we are about to do.

You can check all this out for yourself by looking at Matthew chapter 28, Mark chapter 16, Luke chapter 24, and John chapter 20. What follows is my summary of her evidence as found in those documents.

She was there, at the foot of the cross, when Jesus died. Beside her at the foot of the cross that day were Mary—this one the mother of Jesus—and a young man named John, and several other women. All of them were deeply distraught when, with a great cry, Jesus gave up the ghost, and sagged forward on the cross, clearly dead.

They stayed and watched as the soldiers thrust a spear into his side to ensure that he really was dead. Even after that, Mary stayed at the site of the execution. She was still there when those two wealthy men, Joseph of Arimathea and Nicodemus, came and claimed the body—having first obtained the permission of Governor Pilate. She followed them as they carried the body to a garden not far away, outside the city walls. There was, in that garden, a brand new rock tomb. They laid the body in that tomb and sealed it with a large stone.

She then went back to the house shared by those few disciples who had remained in Jerusalem, and described to them the location of the tomb. Then the sun set, and the Sabbath began. Nothing more could be done until Sabbath was over.

On the Sunday morning, at first light, she left the house and set out for the garden tomb. She didn't wait for the other women who also planned to go to the tomb that morning. But when she got there she found the stone rolled away from the entrance. Her immediate assumption was that someone had stolen the body. She ran all the way back to the house and breathlessly told Peter and John: "They have taken the Lord out of the tomb, and we don't know where they've put him!" (John 20:2).

The two men set off at a run, while Mary followed—but the men ran faster, and rapidly left her behind. By the time she arrived back at the garden both men had gone again.

As she stood outside the tomb crying, she bent down to look into the interior—and got the shock of her life. She saw two men dressed in white. So, who were they? Mary's testimony is that they were angels. They said to her, "Woman, why are you crying?". She must have thought this was a dumb question. It was obvious why she was crying, but she replied politely, "They have taken my Lord away, and I don't know where they have put him" (John 20:13).

No sooner had she said this, than she heard another voice, behind her, asking the same question: "Woman", he said, "why are you crying? Who is it you are looking for?" (John 20:15). And who was this third person? Well, she thought (at first) it was the gardener, and so she said "Sir, if you've carried him away, tell me where you've put him, and I will get him". And then? Then he spoke her name—and she knew it was him . . . she knew it was Jesus. She turned and looked at him, and stepped towards him, but he said, "Do not hold on to me, for I have not yet returned to the Father. Go instead to my brothers and tell them, 'I am returning to my Father and your Father, to my God and your God'" (John 20: 17).

Could she have been mistaken? How certain is she that it was really Jesus? Her testimony makes it clear that she was absolutely certain.

WITNESS: SIMON PETER

The next witness we call to the stand, members of the jury, is Simon Peter. If he was actually in front of us, he would explain that, as he was born in a bilingual region (namely Galilee) there are several forms of his name. In Hebrew he is Simeon bar Jonah (meaning Simon, son of John). Both forms 'Simeon' and 'Simon' would have been used in his bilingual native town of Bethsaida. Then Jesus gave him a new name, in Aramaic (or conversational Hebrew) this was 'Cephas' and in Greek it translated to 'Petros' or 'Peter'. But the double-barreled name of 'Simon Peter' is the one by which he is commonly known.

If we pictured him on the witness stand it would be as a rough, bluff, hearty sort of fellow—someone we would expect to make a good impression on the members of a jury—a blunt spoken north-countryman, a tradesman and businessman, whose family had been associated with the fishing industry in and around Galilee for many generations in both Bethsaida and Capernaum.

But, once again, we must focus not on what we might imagine him to be like, but on the actual evidence the ancient documents record. And, once again, this is found in those four biographies of Jesus: Matthew, Mark, Luke and John. What follows is my summary of what they tell us.

Peter first met Jesus through his brother Andrew (John 1:41). Peter responded to the call to follow Jesus when he heard those famous words, "Follow me" (Mark 1:16, 17).

And Peter came to know Jesus very well indeed. He was one of an inner group, chosen by Jesus to travel with him. Those journeys took them all around Galilee, to Jerusalem and back, and they were with him on that last, awful journey to Jerusalem when Jesus knew that he was travelling to his death. Jesus kept explaining this to them, but they couldn't really understand— not until it happened, that is. What Jesus said to them on that last journey towards Jerusalem was: "the Son of Man did not come to be served, but to serve, and to give his life as a ransom for many" (Mark. 10:45).

We can see, from the testimony of Peter and two letters he wrote, that Peter had vivid and clear memories of his time with Jesus—of all the stories Jesus told, and the great insight and wisdom contained in those stories: great insight into the human heart and into the plans of God. It is also plain that Jesus understood Peter's heart. When Peter was boasting that he would never deny Jesus, would stand by him even at the cost of his own life, Jesus said: "I tell you the truth, Peter, today—yes, tonight—before the rooster crows twice you yourself will disown me three times" (Mark 14:30).

But there was one moment that was a key one for Peter—a moment when it became clear to him who Jesus really was. Peter's Master had just opened the eyes of a blind man, and then, in a sense, opened the 'spiritual eyes' of Peter and the others.

They were walking towards the villages around Caesarea Philippi. On the way Jesus asked, "Who do people say I am?".

They replied, "Some say John the Baptist; others say Elijah; and still others, one of the prophets".

"But", said Jesus, "what about you? Who do you say I am?". Peter answered, "You are the Christ" (Mark 8:27-29).

Now, I put it to you, members of the jury, that the question Jesus asked Peter and his friends is the same question, the same challenge, that faces all of us. If what the Bible says about Jesus is true, then the crucial question is the one that Jesus puts to each of us: "Who do you say that I am?". Consider your answer to that one very carefully, members of the jury, because you are passing judgement on yourselves when you answer. Your answer classifies you, as it were, and upon your answer great things hang—chiefly your own permanent and eternal destiny.

HEARING PETER'S VOICE

One of the hardest tasks for you, and any jury members, is keeping an open mind until you have heard all that a particular witness has to say. Indeed, longer than that—until you have heard all the witnesses and all the evidence.

For our imaginary trial in this book, I can only summarize some of what Peter can tell us about the case currently before the court. I challenge you, members of the jury, to read the full transcript of his evidence for yourselves.

You'll find Peter's account of his time with Jesus recorded, in particular, in the book written by Peter's friend and colleague, Mark. It's called 'Mark's Gospel' and is the second book in the New Testament part of the Bible. It's only short, so lay your hands on a copy of the Bible in modern, easy-to-read English and read it for yourself. Also in the New Testament you'll find (as I mentioned earlier) two short letters written by Peter, and you'll find an account of his role in the very early days of the faith in the book called 'Acts'.

Now, let's return to Simon Peter's evidence, and what it tells us about the final hours of Jesus.

On the night before he died, Jesus went out into a garden in the moonlight to pray. He took Peter, James and John with him to this garden (called Gethsemane) and told them to wait for him while he went a little further on to pray in solitude. Jesus told them to stay awake and alert, but they just couldn't keep their eyes open. When he returned he found them asleep.

Then a mob, of Temple guards, arrived in the garden led by the traitor Judas. They were armed with swords and clubs. They had been sent by the Temple authorities. Judas indicated which one was Jesus and they seized him. His followers fled, but Peter followed the guards at a distance and saw them take their prisoner to the high priest's house.

Jesus was taken inside, and then the guards gathered around an open fire in the courtyard of the house. Peter crept out of the darkness to join them, or at least to warm himself by the blaze. Three times that night Peter's north-country accent was recognized by servants who were passing by or hanging around the fire. Each time they accused Peter of being a follower of Jesus, and each time he denied it. On the third occasion he did this he heard a rooster crowing—crowing for the second time.

It was that dim early light just before dawn, and Peter looked up to see Jesus being led out of the high priest's house. When their eyes met, Peter remembered what Jesus had predicted, and turned and fled in tears.

He remained in hiding all that day and night and the following day. Early on the Sunday morning he was woken by Mary Magdalene who told him and John that the tomb where Jesus had been buried was now empty. In a frantic voice she told them: "They have taken the Lord out of the tomb, and we don't know where they have put him!" (John 20:2). Peter and John were suddenly wide awake. They leapt up and ran for the tomb.

John arrived first, and stood gaping at the opening to the tomb, with its great stone rolled back. Peter stooped and looked inside, but saw only burial clothes lying undisturbed. Then he and John returned to the house wondering what had happened.

Later that day, Peter did see Jesus, and speak to him. Once alone, and on a number of occasions with others present. That very Sunday night in an upper room Jesus came and spoke to Peter and nine of the other leaders who were present. Later they saw him again in Galilee, both by the lake and on the mountain side.

But was it really Jesus? It is clear from the testimony we read that Peter was utterly convinced this was the same Jesus they had followed and known so well for some three years before his death. And Peter explains that death for us: "Christ died for sins once for all, the righteous for the unrighteous, to bring you to God. He was put to death in the body but made alive by the Spirit" (1 Peter 3:18).

A CROWDED
WITNESS STAND

$\mathcal{N}$ow in our examination of those who claim to be witnesses to Jesus—claim to have personally witnessed Jesus alive, fully alive, after his death and burial—we are going to put three women on the witness stand at the same time. The experience they can report is a shared experience. Because this is an informal hearing we will bend the rules, and put all three under oath, and take evidence from all three simultaneously.

Once again, members of the jury, your task is to weigh up their evidence on 'the balance of probabilities'.

Let's introduce these three women to you. The first is another woman named Mary. Among first century Jews 'Mary' or 'Marian' (Greek forms of the Hebrew name "Miriam") was a popular name and was widely used. The source of the name was the original Miriam, the sister of Moses. We've already heard about the Mary who was the mother of Jesus, and we've read the testimony of Mary Magdalene. This one is sometimes called 'the other Mary', sometimes 'Mary the mother of James', and sometimes 'Mary of Clopas' (in other words, the wife of Clopas). She is listed as being among those women who accompanied Jesus to Jerusalem, were present at the crucifixion, and went to the garden tomb on that Sunday morning. On the Friday afternoon this other Mary was with Mary Magdalene when she followed Joseph of Arimathea and Nicodemus, and saw where they buried the body of Jesus.

The second woman is Salome. She is the aunt of Jesus, the sister of his mother Mary. She was married to a man named

Zebedee, and her two sons, James and John, were the cousins of Jesus (as well as being among his followers).

The third woman is named Joanna. She is one of several women healed by Jesus, who assisted in maintaining his itinerant group as they travelled from town to town. Her husband's name was Chuza, and he held an official position on the staff of Herod Antipas, the 'tetrarch' (or ruler) of the regions of Galilee and Peraea.

The story of these three women, as recorded in the New Testament part of the Bible, is as follows.

The women knew that Jesus had been buried by two men, and that this had been done in some haste. During the Sabbath day, that is, during the Saturday, they decided that they would go to the tomb and do whatever had to be done to ensure that the body of Jesus was properly laid out, and treated with spices and ointments (as was normally done in those days). The Sabbath ended at sunset on Saturday, but by then it was too dark to do anything. So it was at first light the next morning that they gathered up their spices and set out for the tomb.

As they neared the garden containing the tomb they realized they had a problem: the huge stone that sealed the tomb entrance. Who would roll that stone away for them? But when they arrived, they found the stone already rolled back, and the tomb standing open. They went in, and found the tomb empty except for the burial shroud—the body was gone.

When they came back out into the garden they saw two men dressed in white. These were angels. The women were frightened, and bowed down, with their faces to the ground. The "men in white" said to them: "Why do you look for the living among the dead? He is not here; he has risen! Remember how he told you, while he was still with you in Galilee: 'The Son of

Man must be delivered into the hands of sinful men, be cruci-fied and on the third day be raised again'" (Luke 24:5-7).

Then they remembered the things that Jesus had said about his death, and about coming back from the dead. In a jumble of emotions that included both fear and joy, they ran back to the house and told the men there what they had seen and heard.

The men were inclined to dismiss their story as nonsense, but Peter and John (as we've already seen) ran to the tomb to check it out. Mary Magdalene ran after them, but the other Mary, Salome and Joanna set off for the nearby village of Bethany to tell the rest of the group their news. On the way to Bethany, they were suddenly and unexpectedly, confronted by Jesus: alive and well, standing in front of them, looking as he had always looked, and sounding as he had always sounded. "Greetings", he said to them. "Don't be afraid. Go and tell my brothers to go to Galilee; there they will see me" (Matthew 28:9-10).

WITNESS: CLEOPAS

The next witness is a man named Cleopas. This is actually a nickname or abbreviation. His full name would have been Cleopatros, but he was known as Cleopas. He was just an ordi-nary follower of Jesus, no-one special, not one of the leadership or inner circle: just an ordinary believer.

He had been in Jerusalem for the Passover Festival, so he was in the city when Jesus was arrested, rushed through a mockery of a trial, and executed. On the Sunday, the day after the Sabbath, and two days after the death and burial, Cleopas and a friend were walking from Jerusalem back to their home village of Emmaus (a journey of some 12 kilometres or so). And what happened on that journey is what makes Cleopas a useful witness for us (you'll find the report of this incident in Luke 24:13-35).

As he and his friend were walking they talked about all that had happened in Jerusalem over the last few days, still being almost in a state of shock over the sudden arrest and execution of Jesus.

There were others on that road that morning, and one of them fell into step beside Cleopas and his friend and asked what they were talking about. Cleopas responded: "Are you only a visitor to Jerusalem and don't know the things that have happened there in these days?" (Luke 24:18). He went on to explain that he meant those events concerning Jesus of Nazareth, adding that he was:

> a prophet strong in what he did and what he said, in God's eyes as well as the people's. Haven't you heard how our Chief Priests and rulers handed him over for execution, and had him crucified? But we were hoping he was the one who was to come and set Israel free...Yes, and as if that were not enough, it's getting on for three days since all this happened; and some of our women folk have disturbed us deeply. For they went to the tomb at dawn, and then when they couldn't find his body they said that they had had a vision of angels who said that he was alive. Some of our people went straight off to the tomb and found things just as the women had described them—but they didn't see *him*! (Luke 24:19-24, Phillips).

The stranger responded to this outburst by criticizing them for not understanding the nature of God's rescue mission to Planet Earth. He went on to show them from the oldest parts of the Bible that all these things that happened were exactly what were meant to happen, what had to happen, for God's plans to be fulfilled.

When the three of them reached the village of Emmaus it was getting close to sunset, and Cleopas invited the stranger to come in and join them for a meal. He accepted the invitation. Food was spread on the table, and then Cleopas invited the obviously well-educated stranger to say the blessing over the food. When he did this, Cleopas and his friend suddenly and abruptly recognized who this man was—it was Jesus. And just as they recognized him, he was gone, and there were only two of them in the room.

The room was then empty of this powerful presence and Cleopas and his friend, even though it was now dark, rushed back those 12 kilometres to Jerusalem, to report their experience to the others.

Part 2

TIME
OUT TO
CONSIDER

*L*et us pause for a moment to collate the evidence we have heard so far.

The evidence we have been considering has been to do with the appearances of the risen, living Jesus after his death and burial. Those early Christian documents, collected together in the New Testament part of the Bible, record at least eleven separate appearances by Jesus.

First, there's the appearance to Mary Magdalene in the
garden early on the Sunday morning;
second to the group of women on the same morning;
third to the two travellers on the road to Emmaus;
fourth to Peter in Jerusalem at some time during that
same Sunday;
fifth, to ten disciples in the upper room that Sunday night;
sixth, to eleven of them a week later;
seventh, to a group of some seven of those disciples on
the shore of Lake Galilee;
eighth, to eleven disciples on a mountain side in Galilee;
ninth, at the same place some time later to more than 500
people at once;
tenth, to James, the brother of Jesus;
and eleventh, the final appearance to a large group of early
Christian leaders on the Mount of Olives.

These appearances were spread over a period of 40 days. This, as you can see from the list, is no small, or rare, occurrence— but a repeated occurrence, before different witnesses at different places and in different settings. There is no stereotyped repetition here. And then, several years later, there was one twelfth, and last, appearance, to Paul on the road to Damascus. (We'll have a look at that appearance later.)

The written reports of these appearances, collected in the New Testament part of the Bible, are for the most part reports from people who claim to be eyewitnesses to these events—who claim to be reporting what they have seen and heard. This sort of claim has legal standing and must be taken seriously. When living witnesses are not available (not after 2,000 years) then it is right and proper for a court to take "written evidence" from such witnesses.

If the question was raised by the complainant in this civil action (the complainant is the one objecting to the truth about Jesus) then the respondent could refer to the American case, *Dallas County v Commercial Union Assurance Company*. In that trial, a newspaper article was produced as evidence—a newspaper article that was 58 years old. The journalist who wrote it was dead, and only his written, published account was available. But that article claimed to be an eyewitness account of a particular fire. The written article was accepted, even though the journalist who wrote it was not there to take the oath and swear to the truth of the article in court.

And did that court do the right thing in accepting a "written witness" in place of a living one? The Federal Court of Appeal said it was perfectly correct to do so. Here is part of what the Appeal Court said in its judgement: "To our minds, the article published in the *Selma Morning Times* on the day of the fire is more reliable, more trustworthy, more competent evidence than the testimony of a witness called 58 years later".

The same holds true for these reports of Jesus coming back from the dead. They date from the correct time period, and come from people who are likely to be eyewitnesses, and who claim to be eyewitnesses. On the balance of probabilities it is reasonable to accept them. And they must be given far greater weight than those critics who allege they are false or mistaken, critics who are writing not a mere 58 years later, but some 2,000 years later. Legal precedent says that it is reasonable to accept those written witnesses and reject the modern critics—indeed, it is unreasonable to do otherwise.

∾

ALLOWING FOR
ALL THE POSSIBILITIES

Remember, members of the jury, that earlier I quoted leading British lawyer Sir Norman Anderson as saying: "The account should be accepted as *prima facie* reliable unless there is evidence to show that the opposite is the case".

Some people are going to object that there *is* evidence to show these supposed eyewitness reports are unreliable—and that evidence, they will claim, is the fact that the eyewitnesses claim to report supernatural events. As an example, take the references to angels.

My dictionary defines 'angel' as meaning 'spiritual beings, messengers from God'—and asking anyone living in the age of science and technology to believe in such beings is like asking them to believe in little green men or bug-eyed monsters from outer space. Therefore, the critics want to conclude, the presence of angels in these narratives makes them inherently unlikely.

So, let me respond to that argument.

In the first place, there seem to be a lot of people these days, including a lot of highly respected scientists, who are very ready to believe in "little green men or bug-eyed monsters from outer space"—at least in some form or another. It is high-powered scientists who are behind the SETI project. That stands for 'Search for Extra Terrestrial Intelligence'.

Quite a lot of good research money is being spent on radio telescopes that sweep the night sky listening for the sounds of transmissions whose regularity and pattern show them to be the product of intelligence. Note that they are not just searching for life in outer space—such as single celled microbes or bacteria—but *intelligence*: beings developed enough, and creative enough, that their alien civilization is producing recognizable transmissions. And from time to time one leading scientist or another will write an article for a popular magazine or newspaper arguing that there *must* be intelligent life out there, in the stars, somewhere: and doing the mathematics to support their argument.

If, in this age of science and technology, scientists want us to believe in alien intelligence beyond our solar system based on guess-work and mathematics, it is just as reasonable to accept the existence of angels based on well-attested eyewitness reports that corroborate each other. The scientists' proposition is already accepting that this universe is a stranger place than we had once imagined, and that it may be inhabited by strange beings, well beyond our normal experience—therefore, it is reasonable to extend this notion of possible inhabitants of creation to include angels as well as aliens.

When it comes to angels, the first thing to do is to try to dismiss all the Hollywood ideas, and cartoonists' drawings, and all the cultural gloss that has been put on the word. Forget wings, and harps, and visual splendour and weird beings with magical powers. The word 'angel' just means, literally, 'messenger'.

We have earlier talked about the fact that the universe is more than matter—that the strictly materialistic account of the universe is inadequate and unconvincing. Once we have granted that there is another realm—call it 'second nature' or 'supernature' or simply the non-physical realm—there is no reason to assume that this other realm should not have inhabitants (including conscious, intelligent inhabitants) just as our realm has.

This is no bigger an assumption than the assumption underlying SETI—which is that other stars may well have planets that support intelligent life. Once we acknowledge the enormity of the universe (in both its physical and non-physical dimensions), and how much of it remains unknown to us, the notion of intelligent inhabitants of that other realm is clearly not unreasonable.

It is really only the *word* 'angel' that makes us uncomfortable. And we should not let a word get in the way of our search for the truth about Jesus. The claim the Bible makes is that these beings from the realm of supernature can be, and sometimes are, sent as messengers by the Creator God, the maker and controller of all realms of existence—and that certain of these beings were so employed at the special moment when supernature was dramatically invading nature in the resurrection of Jesus from the dead.

We are once again back at the old problem of not letting our prejudice, or bias, or emotion, close our minds to what, on the balance of probabilities, is entirely reasonable.

A QUESTION
OF CONTRADICTIONS

$\mathcal{M}$embers of the jury, having got this far in our investigation of the truth about Jesus—who he was and what happened to him—it seems to be that the 'balance of probabilities' (to use the legal phrase) leans heavily towards this remarkable fact that Jesus appears to have come back from the dead.

But, then, of course, I would say that, since I am the counsel for the respondent in this civil court action we are imagining.

Others will remain a long way short of being persuaded just yet. And it is to some of the objections they raise that I now turn, before calling further eyewitness evidence.

For example, one objection that is raised is that the four short biographies of Jesus (known as the Gospels of Matthew, Mark, Luke and John) contain minor variations, and that these minor variations amount to being contradictions. Now, if they really do contradict one another that is important, and it will diminish, or dismiss entirely, the claim of these documents to provide eyewitness evidence.

Lawyer and Baptist minister Ross Clifford tells this story: "I was involved in a case where two policemen, prosecution witnesses, lied. To support their claim, they invented a story about a motor vehicle they alleged was involved in the incident. The truth of the matter was this vehicle did not exist. In cross examination their case was annihilated as they contradicted each other over the make, model and colour of the mystery car".

Is that sort of flat out contradiction what we find in the New

Testament documents?

No, it is not. It's as simple as that, really.

It is not the case that one report says Jesus died in Jerusalem, and another says he died in Nazareth. It is not the case that one report says Jesus was crucified and another says he was stoned to death. It is not the case that one report says Jesus was sentenced by the Roman governor and another report says the Roman governor played no role. You can hunt through the New Testament documents and there simply aren't any flat out contradictions of that sort to be found. They just aren't there.

I have occasionally had someone say to me, "Ah, but those reports about Jesus are full of contradictions", to which I respond: "Name one"—and they can't. They make their claim based on something that someone told them once that they had heard from someone else.

This is exactly what a member of the jury (such as yourself) must not do. Never accept second, third and fourth hand hearsay assumptions and presuppositions. Insist on going to the source documents, on reading those source documents for yourself, and deciding on the words you can read with your own eyes, and not on the basis what someone says the words say.

More than that, those four biographies of Jesus, far from *contradicting* each other, actually *complement* each other. That is to say, that one fills in the details another leaves out. Here is one quick example.

Matthew, Mark, Luke and John all agree that Jesus was rushed through a hurried and hasty trial before the Temple authorities. It is clear, from all four reports, that this trial was not conducted in a cool and legal way, but as an angry and abusive assault on the prisoner (the sort of thing that happens under repressive dictatorships). Which is why we read about this rather nasty little incident during the trial: "they spat in his face and struck him with their fists. Others slapped him and said, 'Prophesy to us, Christ. Who hit you?'" (Matthew 26:67-68).

When you read that in Matthew you think: what an odd question to ask. Why did they imagine there was any point in asking Jesus who had hit him, since he had just seen who had done it? But Luke, in his account, fills in additional details and makes it clear. Luke records the incident in these words: "They blindfolded him and demanded, 'Prophesy! Who hit you?'" (Luke 22:64). Ah, so they blindfolded Jesus first, before they hit him! That explains exactly what was happening.

And that is typical of the way these four short biographies of Jesus fit together: they *complement* each other.

Nevertheless, while it is true that Matthew, Mark, Luke and John never flat-out contradict each other, and that (on the whole) they complement each other, isn't it true that there are minor variations in their reports? Yes, it is perfectly true. And all the legal authorities say that minor variations between witnesses are evidence of *truth* not *falsehood*.

Imagine a car accident that happens at an intersection, and imagine further that there are four eyewitnesses—one standing on each corner of the intersection. Each witness sees the same accident, but each sees it from a slightly different angle. So, although the four different testimonies harmonize and complement each other, they are not identical—there are minor variations.

In that sort of situation, if all four witnesses gave identical testimony, in almost identical words, the presiding judge would be suspicious that the witnesses had colluded together, that they had rehearsed their evidence, and that, as a result, their evidence was 'contaminated' (that's the legal term) and could not be trusted. It might even indicate a conspiracy between the witnesses.

That is why minor variations are evidence of truth, not falsehood. Minor variations are normal and natural, and are to be expected when you are hearing from real witnesses to real events.

The minor variations (and they are very minor) that we find in Matthew, Mark, Luke and John are evidence that we are reading real witnesses to a real situation: that the reports are true, not false.

Lawyers call this process of drawing together the evidence from different witnesses 'harmonization'—and careful reading of the four short biographies of Jesus in the New Testament shows that they harmonize, complementing each other with exactly those small, minor variations that are to be expected in genuine witnesses.

Here's an example of just such a 'minor variation'. In Matthew 27:15-17 we read: "it was the governor's custom at the Feast to release a prisoner chosen by the crowd. At that time they had a notorious prisoner, called Barabbas. So when the crowd had gathered, Pilate asked them, 'Which one do you want me to release to you: Barabbas, or Jesus who is called Christ?'" (The crowd, as you know if you've read the story, cry out that they want Barabbas released.) Who exactly was Barabbas? The accounts differ slightly, and this is the kind of 'minor variation' we get. Matthew and John both described Barabbas as "a notorious prisoner", while Mark and Luke add the additional detail that Barabbas was what we would today call a terrorist: "A man called Barabbas was in prison with the insurrectionists who had committed murder in the uprising" (Mark 15:7) and "Now Barabbas had taken part in a rebellion" (John 18:40).

These additional details are the minor variations that complement one another, and show us that we are here reading reliable evidence, taken from eyewitnesses.

Here's another example: the Roman governor (Pontius Pilate) arranged for a notice to be placed on the cross on which Jesus was executed. There are very slight variations in the way that the four biographers of Jesus record the words on that notice. Matthew records it (27:37) as "THIS IS JESUS, THE KING OF THE JEWS". Mark (15:26) says it read: "THE KING OF THE JEWS". Luke records (23:38) it as, "THE KING OF THE JEWS", and John (19:19) as "JESUS OF NAZARETH, THE KING OF THE JEWS".

Now, is there any flat out contradiction as to fact there? No, there's not. Is it just the sort of minor variation that would give a judge confidence in the reliability of the witnesses? Yes, that's exactly what it is.

Let me draw these threads together by taking you back to the end of the 19th century and introducing you to a man named Sir Robert Anderson. He was Assistant Commissioner of Scotland Yard and a trained lawyer. Anderson was also a thoughtful and intelligent Christian who wrote a book entitled *A Doubter's Doubts About Science and Religion*. Here is the conclusion that he reached: the reports of Matthew, Mark, Luke and John, he said, "would be accepted as valid by any fair tribunal in the world". And, he added, the resurrection, "is a public fact accredited by evidence which will stand the test of discussion and verification".

∾

OBJECTION, YOUR HONOUR!

*F*or the moment in our trial, I have turned from the evidence and the witnesses to consider some of the objections that opponents of Jesus and the Bible have been dying to raise ever since I started presenting this case. And considering serious objections means returning to a group I mentioned once before: namely "The Jesus Seminar".

For more than a decade now much of the media discussion of Jesus (who he is, and what happened to him) has been dominated by this group. And this didn't happen by mistake—part of the agenda of this group is to attempt to dominate media discussion of Jesus. Their stated aim is to change what people have believed about Jesus for the past 2,000 years.

This self-appointed group has announced their mission as being "to wrestle the popular perception of Jesus from fundamentalists who control the religious airwaves". Their problem is that the evidence is lining up in favor of those so-called "fundamentalists." ('Fundamentalist' is one of those journalistic code words that means 'ignorant bigot'. The cheapest and least intelligent way of disposing of your opponent's argument is to label him a 'fundamentalist'. Since the members of "The Jesus Seminar" claim to be scholars it is disappointing to see them resorting to such hysterical, unscholarly language.)

One participant in the Seminar is a man named John Dominic Crossan. He teaches at De Paul University in the United States. He argues against the sort of case that I (as the counsel for the respondent in this court) have been building up. Crossan claims that the Gospels (those biographies of Jesus by Matthew, Mark,

Luke and John) are mere propaganda written long after the time of Jesus by men who never knew Jesus. As such, claims Crossan, their reports cannot be relied upon as history.

So, does John Dominic Crossan's claim stand up to close, critical and historical examination?

No, it does not.

So far I have shown that those New Testament documents come through historical tests extremely well. The 'balance of probabilities' (our legal standard of proof) tells us that we should take the New Testament seriously as reliable historical evidence. What does the same sort of test tell us when we apply it to the claims of John Dominic Crossan? The test of history flat out refutes Crossan and shows his claims are false.

Here is one example. Crossan argues that when the Gospels describe the empty tomb of Jesus, they aren't describing an actual event. He claims that nothing like what they describe was even possible. This whole account of the body of Jesus being buried in a borrowed rock tomb is so unlikely, Crossan insists, that it must be dismissed out of hand as a late myth—a mere invention. This, of course, is a very serious charge, and it has to be seriously considered. So what does Crossan claim happened to Jesus' body? If Jesus did not come back from the dead, we are back with the old problem: why didn't his enemies produce his body after stories of the resurrection began to spread? Not having any historical evidence to support his claims, and being reduced to speculation, Crossan speculates (that's a polite way of saying that he guesses) that wild dogs probably ate the body of Jesus.

The heart of Crossan's claim is that crucified criminals were *never* buried in the manner described in the Gospels. That's what he says—never. Rather, he says, their bodies were always thrown into a common grave—in the valley of Hinnom, just south of the city of Jerusalem—where animals could get to them. Rubbish was burned in Hinnom, and wild animals scavenged there for food. And that's where the body of Jesus was thrown, and that's what happened to it. So, at least, is the claim that Crossan makes.

Now, remember he has no evidence to support his claim at all—not one scrap of evidence. He bases this story on his claim that crucified men were *never* buried in rock tombs.

But now some solid historical evidence has emerged that we can test Crossan's claim against: and it fails the test. You see, archaeologists recently discovered the remains of a crucified man, dating from around the time of Jesus, who had been buried in much the same manner as the gospels describe. So John Dominic Crossan should, at this stage, retire from the courtroom looking embarrassed. So much for his claim that crucified men were *never* buried in rock tombs. So much for his wild guesses about wild dogs!

Archaeology—in other words, solid, physical evidence—has proved embarrassing for critics of Jesus and the Bible more than once. People like the "Jesus Seminar" keep being exposed by archaeological facts. They cook up theories based on their opposition to Jesus and the Bible, and publish their theories in books and articles, and then they are overtaken by archaeological evidence.

Here's another example. Until five years ago, many of these critics said they doubted the reports of Jesus' trial before the Temple authorities.

The body before whom Jesus was put on trial was called the Sanhedrin. This was the name for the highest tribunal of the authorities in ancient Judea. The word 'Sanhedrin' itself might be translated as 'council'. So, perhaps one way to imagine it would be as a local governing body sitting as a magistrate's court—it's that sort of thing. There were certain procedures that were meant to be followed. The Sanhedrin sat in a semicircle and had two clerks of court, one to record votes of acquittal, and the other votes of condemnation. Arguments for acquittal were presented first, and then those for condemnation. If a witness gave evidence for acquittal he was not allowed to change his mind later, but if someone spoke for condemnation they were allowed to change their mind later and favour acquittal, if they wished. There were detailed rules about how many witnesses were needed to bring about a condemnation of the accused, how many made up a quorum of the court, and so on. In this regard, the legality of the trial of Jesus has been discussed by many writers, and it's fairly clear there are elements about it which point in the direction of a miscarriage of justice.

The reason this trial interested the opponents of Jesus and the Bible is that the New Testament documents say that the man who was High Priest at the time, and supervised the trial, was named Caiaphas. The critics leaped gleefully on this. They claimed there was no evidence, outside the New Testament, that there had ever been a high priest named Caiaphas.

Then, in 1995, workers excavating outside Jerusalem came across a burial cave. Inside the cave was a casket marked "Joseph, the son of Caiaphas". Scholars soon concluded that the Caiaphas in the inscription was the same one referred to in the Gospels.

Archaeological confirmation of the New Testament isn't limited to historical figures like Caiaphas.

Scientists have discovered that the desire of writers such as

Matthew, Mark, Luke and John to spread the good news about Jesus didn't prevent them from accurately portraying first-century Palestine. All the small details, it turns out, are exactly right.

Mendel Nun, an Israeli archaeologist, told the journal *Biblical Archeology Review* that he was continually surprised at how accurately the New Testament writers "reflect natural phenomena around the Sea of Galilee".

And so it goes on, with the evidence of archaeology supporting the evidence of history already cited in this case. Excavations have uncovered what some scholars believe is the home of Peter in Bethsaida—the place that Jesus used as his headquarters when he was in the Galilee region. Excavations in and around Bethsaida have confirmed the portrait of the region presented in the gospels.

Discoveries like these are a powerful rebuke to those who, like the "Jesus Seminar", maintain that the Bible writers distort or misrepresent history. The distortion and misrepresentation comes from the critics, and not from the Bible. That should come as no surprise, since the Bible makes specific historical claims about Jesus. For the first followers of Jesus, history was an inseparable part of his story—not something they made up to suit their purposes. Their commitment to history has been confirmed by archaeologists.

A FURTHER OBJECTION

*M*embers of the jury, we are considering the objections that get raised today to the story of Jesus—who he is, and what happened to him.

There is one general objection that is so vague and general that it is very hard to address. Nonetheless, it is such a common objection that I have to try to find a way to summarize it and respond to it.

This objection goes something like this: there must be something fundamentally wrong with Jesus, or wrong with the records we have about him, or wrong with those people who claim to follow him, because so much evil has been done in his name.

According to one estimate, some 160 million people have been killed violently in wars and genocide in the 2,000 years since the time of Jesus. And, so this objection goes, the influence of Jesus in history seems to have done little to stop the killing. Religious conflicts, according to this objection, are the source of massacres.

The evidence that is cited includes things like the Crusades. These were a series of military expeditions launched by the Christian West between AD 1095 and 1291 with the aim of recovering the Holy Land from the Muslims and establishing Christian rule there. Popes preached support for the Crusades, financed them, sent legates to lead them, and indulged even those who pillaged towns and massacred women and children in the name of Jesus—notably in the sacking of Constantinople in 1203.

Then there was the little matter of the Inquisition. This was an ecclesiastical tribunal set up in the 13th century by Pope Gregory IX with a threefold aim: to investigate the spread of heresy; to summon before it all Roman Catholics suspected of heresy; and to show them their errors, punish them and call them to repentance. It was not intended for the conversion of Jews, Muslims and other non-Roman Catholics. The power of the inquisitors, most of them Dominicans or Franciscans, was great, and some were notorious for their cruelty. The use of torture was sanctioned by Pope Innocent IV in 1252. In Spain in the latter 15th century the Spanish Inquisition sought to counter apostate former Jews and Muslims, heretics, and those accused of sorcery and witchcraft.

The witchcraft trials in Salem, Massachusetts, in the United States, and elsewhere in the 17th century are also blamed on the influence of Jesus. And then, coming down to the present day, these same objectors to Jesus point to the tensions that have taken many lives in Northern Ireland and similar trouble spots, and conclude that the less the world hears about Jesus the better.

How can we respond to this objection?

It seems to me that a huge amount of evil and wickedness has been done in this world by many individuals, and many groups, and many nations over many centuries—and they have given a host of different reasons for what they have done.

From Genghis Khan and his invading hordes, to the Huns who sacked ancient Rome, to the brutal terror of the French Revolution (with its 'Madame Guillotine'), to the fear inspired by the evil Gestapo (Hitler's secret police), to the millions who died under communism, to the terrorists who hijacked airliners and flew them into the Pentagon and the World Trade Centre Towers—the list could go on and on, from the dawn of human history to the present day.

These evil people gave many reasons for the violence they

committed—sometimes it was simple greed and gain, sometimes it was inspired (so they said) by nationalism and patriotism, sometimes by a great ideology.

It seems to me that all these things are excuses. Human beings do evil things because there is a shadow of corruption over the human heart. Human beings behave wickedly because they are capable of wicked behaviour.

The excuses they give are just that—excuses. They hurt, conquer, terrorize, rape and pillage *because they want to*. And that's the truth. Then they come up with whatever excuse they think can justify the horrors they have done. If they think they can get away with brutality in the name of nationalism they will. And, sadly, if they think they can get away with brutality in the name of Jesus, they will do that too. But their actions tell us more about them, and more about the human heart, than about Jesus and the Bible.

This kind of argument ("Look at the horrors that have been done in the name of Jesus") should not distract us from Jesus himself.

Imagine a brilliant, gentle, kind surgeon who saves many lives by his surgical skill. This surgeon has a receptionist who is, to put it politely, an old dragon. She is short-tempered, rude and bullying. Because he is rather absent-minded, and distracted, and out of touch with mundane things, the surgeon doesn't know how horrible she is to his patients. Or maybe he does know, and is trying to get her to reform. Perhaps there are reasons why he feels he shouldn't sack the woman (she is the sole support of sick, elderly parents, or something of that sort). And perhaps the surgeon tries to counterbalance his receptionist's bad behaviour by being even nicer himself to his patients. A strange situation, but not impossible to imagine. In that situation, to what extent should you blame the surgeon for his receptionist's behaviour? The fact is, that both are adults, and each is responsible for themselves, and not for the other. The surgeon is responsible for his own behaviour, and we must judge him on that, and the receptionist is responsible for her own behaviour—and she is the one our judgement must focus on in her case.

Something similar might be said about people who behave badly in the name of Jesus. They are responsible for their own actions, and cannot blame how they behave on Jesus or on anyone else.

Whatever we think of Karl Marx's peculiar political theories (nowadays thoroughly discredited, I would have thought) we cannot hold Marx responsible for the megalomania of Joseph Stalin. Stalin must stand in the dock for Stalin's own actions—and he cannot blame someone else, not even Karl Marx, for his brutality and the terror he brought upon his own people.

Again something similar can be said in the case of Jesus and the cruel, evil and brutal men who have behaved with abominable wickedness, and claimed they were doing so in the interests of Jesus. Such men stand alone in the dock, and must take responsibility for their own actions. They cannot shift the blame to anyone else—most certainly not to Jesus.

The hard facts are these—that the black pages of human history teach us there is something fundamentally wrong with the human heart.

G. K. Chesterton once said that human nature is not basically good (as the sentimentalists insist), nor is it basically evil (as the cynics sneeringly claim), rather it is *a good thing gone bad*—made good, and become corrupt. Anything that is good in human nature, says Chesterton, is like the goods Robinson Crusoe had on his island with him: just bits saved from a wreckage. And that wreckage was the decision by the human race to try to run this world themselves—or, rather, ourselves (we're not off the hook on this one)—rather than submit to the rule, and control and direction of the Creator God of the Universe.

Unplugged from God, we are like unplugged appliances—we don't work right. This is that mysterious something that is wrong at the very heart of human nature. And this is exactly what Jesus came to cure.

Jesus came to re-establish our connection to God. That was his mission. Jesus himself described his own mission in these terms: he had come, he said, "to seek and to save what was lost" (Luke 19:10). What was lost was our connection with God, our place in paradise, and our ability to know and do the right. Jesus came to seek and to save us. And it cost him his life—as he always knew it would.

His story is also our story—yours and mine. Furthermore, Jesus cannot be held responsible for what people do in the name of religion—because he is opposed to religion (he calls it 'idolatry'). Jesus is not interested in religion, but in relationship. That is something we will never understand until we have sorted out our own relationship with him.

Part 3

BACK TO
THE CASE

WITNESS: THOMAS

*N*ow, members of the jury, having considered a number of objections, let's return for the moment to the task in hand—namely calling witnesses and assessing their testimony.

And at this point in the proceedings I call Thomas to the stand.

This man was one of the first followers of Jesus—and part of the inner group called 'The Twelve'. His name comes from an Aramaic word meaning 'twin'. Who his twin brother or sister was, we don't know, because that information is not in the Bible. In our English language we have the expression 'Doubting Thomas'—you may have heard the expression from time to time. Well, this man is the particular Thomas from whom we get that expression—as you'll see shortly.

Thomas appears to be a man of some courage. When a friend of Jesus, named Lazarus, died, Jesus announced his intention of returning to Judea. The other disciples reminded him there were people in Judea who wanted to stone him to death. When Jesus insisted on going, it was Thomas who said to the others, "Let us also go, that we may die with him" (John 11:16).

Thomas was also an honest man—he was prepared to speak out and admit when he didn't understand something, rather than hold his peace and pretend to understand what he didn't. And as you and I know from our own experience, that is a hard thing to do. It happened at a time when Jesus was gently breaking the news to Thomas and the rest that what was facing him at Jerusalem was death. It was the same occasion when he warned Peter that his courage would fail, and he would deny him three times. Jesus ended by saying: "Do not let your hearts be troubled. Trust in God; trust also in me. In my Father's house are many rooms; if it were not so, I would have told you. I am going there to prepare a place for you. And if I go and prepare a place for you, I will come back and take you to be with me that you also may be where I am" (John 14:1-3). It was Thomas who spoke up and said, "Lord, we don't know where you are going, so how can we know the way?" (John 14:5).

There is something attractive about someone who is prepared to speak up and speak his mind in that blunt sort of way. In reply, Jesus made that famous remark: "I am the way and the truth and the life. No one comes to the Father except through me" (John 14:6).

But none of these are the things for which Thomas is most famous, nor are they the reason we need to consider his evidence.

On the Sunday when Jesus' tomb was found to be empty, and the living Jesus appeared to a number of the followers, he appeared (that night) to ten disciples in an upper room—but Thomas was not there. As you would expect, the other disciples told him excitedly, "We have seen the Lord!" (John 20:25). But Thomas was not impressed. His response was very much the same as yours might have been, ladies and gentlemen of the jury. Instead, Thomas said to them, "Unless I see the nail marks in his hands and put my finger where the nails were, and put my hand into his side, I will not believe it" (John 20:25).

It is because of that remark that this expression 'Doubting Thomas' has entered our language. Every time you use that expression, this is the man you are referring to.

Let's get our evidence from the historical documents first hand, as it were. Here is the important incident that we want to focus on, as recorded in John's gospel:

Now Thomas (called the Twin), one of the Twelve, was not with the disciples when Jesus came. So the other disciples told him, "We have seen the Lord!". But he said to them, "Unless I see the nail marks in his hands and put my finger where the nails were, and put my hand into his side, I will not believe it". A week later his disciples were in the house again, and Thomas was with them. Though the doors were locked, Jesus came and stood among them and said, "Peace be with you!" Then he said to Thomas, "Put your finger here; see my hands. Reach out your hand and put it into my side. Stop doubting and believe". Thomas said to him, "My Lord and my God!". Then Jesus told him, "Because you have seen me, you have believed; blessed are those who have not seen and yet have believed" (John 20:24-29).

The very fact that this story is recorded at all is further evidence of the honesty and reliability of these records in the New Testament part of the Bible.

This is one of the leaders of the early Christians, being shown at something a great deal less than his best—as a victim of doubt in the face of the central and most dramatic act in God's intervention in human history. But instead of suppressing this story as shameful, it is honestly recorded. If impostors and deceivers had compiled the Bible for their own advantage, they would never have told the world that one of the first founders of the new faith behaved as Thomas behaves here. Likewise, if the Bible was a later invention, this is the sort of incident that would have been 'airbrushed out' to make the picture nicer. Instead of which, this early historical document honestly records Thomas' initial unbelief. (Just as it also records the painful truth about Peter's denial of Jesus at the time Jesus was on trial for his life. This book, the Bible, is painfully honest about all these matters.)

There are several things, members of the jury, I would have you notice about Thomas.

The first is how natural and normal Thomas' response was, certainly for a person of his temperament. It was a genuine response. Despite the fact that the people who told him that Jesus had come from the dead were his friends, people he had travelled with for several years, and (as far as we can tell) people he both liked and admired—he still expressed this sort of gloomy doubt. This, surely, disposes of the silly idea that the first followers of Jesus were gullible, simple minded men who were only too ready to believe anything. Far from being gullible, Thomas expressed the deepest doubts—and there's no record here of the others giving him a hard time over his doubts. They seemed to understand exactly how hard this new development was for anyone to take in. Thomas is not unique, and his wanting to be persuaded is nowhere reprimanded.

In fact, the second thing we can take note of in this report is the gentle way in which Jesus deals with doubt. Jesus realized Thomas's need and offered him evidence. Thomas, of course, is simply overwhelmed by the presence of Jesus. You will have noticed that he never does what he said he had to do: he never does touch the wounds to convince himself they are real, and this is really Jesus. The presence of the living Jesus is just so overwhelming that he doesn't need to. I suspect that, in the end, this is true for all of us—talking to Jesus, being aware of his presence, reading the Bible and finding Jesus striding powerfully and purposefully off its pages is so overwhelming that our doubts are dealt with in a moment.

And finally, members of the jury, notice what Jesus says about us—about you and me. We are the people he is referring to when he says: "blessed are those who have not seen and yet have believed" (John 20:29). In other words, when Jesus asks us to believe—we who were not there in the first century, to gather the evidence of our own eyes—he knows exactly what he is asking, and knows that it's possible, and that it's good for us (a blessing, in fact). If the 'inner eyes' of your understanding can now see what your physical eyes cannot (we're in the wrong time and place for that): then Jesus approves.

∽

WITNESS: PAUL

*M*embers of the jury, I will now summon another witness—in one sense, the most unusual witness of all. Because this man saw the living Jesus, after he had come back from the dead, some time after everybody else had seen him.

The New Testament is not always careful to explain the precise chronology of the events it records. Nevertheless we can say that about a year after Jesus died (and that means about a year after he had appeared, post-mortem, to a large number of his followers) he appeared also to this man we are about to hear from now.

His name is Paul—or, at least, that's what it became. But when he was born he was given the name 'Saul'—most probably being named after his father or some other close male relative, or possibly even after the famous Old Testament figure King Saul, who like Paul was from the tribe of Benjamin. Being born in a Roman city and claiming Roman citizenship, Paul was his official Roman name (in Latin *Paulos*). Tarsus, the place of Paul's birth, was, at the time, the capital of the Roman province of Cilicia, and is still a bustling city a few miles inland from the Mediterranean on Turkey's southern shore. In Paul's day it was a self-governing city, loyal to the Roman Empire.

Growing up in a Jewish family meant that Paul was well trained in the Jewish Scriptures and traditions, beginning in the home with the celebration of the Jewish holy days. At an early age he entered the synagogue day school. There he learned to read and write by copying selected passages from the Bible. He learned the ancient Hebrew language from the Old Testament part of the Bible. At home his parents probably spoke the common dialect of the time—called Aramaic. As Paul related to the larger community, he learned the Greek language. Every Jewish boy also learned a trade. Paul learned the art of tent making which he later used to earn his living. Paul eventually went to Jerusalem to study under the famous rabbi, Gamaliel—the best Jewish teacher of that day.

Paul became very zealous for the traditions of his people. He became, in fact, 'enemy number one' for the first followers of Jesus. He was convinced that those early believers were corrupting the faith and traditions that he held in such high regard, and so he began persecuting them.

But in the middle of his passionate, angry persecution of the early Christians he was confronted by the risen, living Jesus and his whole life was turned around. But let's turn to the historical documents, and read Paul's words for ourselves:

> I am a Jew, born in Tarsus, a city in Cilicia, but educated in Jerusalem under Gamaliel, at whose feet I learned to follow our Jewish laws and customs very carefully. I became very anxious to honour God in everything I did. And I persecuted the Christians, hounding them to death, binding and delivering both men and women to prison. The High Priest or any member of the council can testify that this is so. For I asked them for letters to the Jewish leaders in Damascus, with instructions to let me bring any Christians I found to Jerusalem in chains to be punished. As I was on the road, nearing Damascus, suddenly about noon a very bright light from heaven shone around me.
>
> And I fell to the ground, and heard a voice saying to me, "Saul, Saul, why are you persecuting me?".
>
> "Who is speaking to me, sir?" I asked.
>
> And he replied, "I am Jesus of Nazareth, the one you are persecuting".
>
> The men with me saw the light but didn't understand what was said.
>
> And I said, "What shall I do, Lord?".
>
> And the Lord told me, "Get up and go into Damascus, and there you will be told what awaits you in the years ahead".
>
> I was blinded by the intense light, and had to be led into Damascus by my companions.
>
> There a man named Ananias, as godly a man as you could find for obeying the law, and well thought of by all the Jews of Damascus, came to me, and standing beside me said, "Brother Saul, receive your sight!".

And that very hour I could see him!

Then he told me, "The God of our fathers has chosen you to know his will and to see the Messiah and hear him speak. You will take his message everywhere, telling what you have seen and heard" (Acts 22:3-15 *The Living Bible*).

For all the reports we read, Paul makes a good impression. He strikes us as a man of character and confidence—as a man of intelligence and integrity—and yet he tells this bizarre story. Bright light on the road to Damascus...a voice that spoke to Paul...Paul going temporarily blind...having his sight restored. It sounds like a fairy tale. But when we say that, is it our reason speaking, or our narrow minded prejudice?

Certainly it is the sort of thing that doesn't appear to happen today. At best, it might be described as a very rare and special event in human history. It is most certainly not the sort of thing that is part of our common or daily experience. But is that any reason to dismiss it out of hand as impossible? Unlikely things do happen. Statistically rare things do happen.

So, might this unusual, even unique, event have actually occurred in just the way that Paul described it?

Your answer to that will be determined by whether you have ruled out the possibility that the Creator God exists, and is capable of special (even spectacular) interventions in human affairs. If you are a hard-line materialist, rejecting the existence of anything you cannot perceive with your senses, then you will reject this account. You must.

However, if you are open to the possibility that there is a realm beyond our immediate, mundane experience—a non-physical realm—then you cannot simply dismiss this story, just because it is unlike any experience you have ever had.

Perhaps God gave this man this experience so that he could tell you about it—so that he could become a mouthpiece for God, a spokesman for God, *to you*. If that is the plan, if that is the intention, you would be smart to listen to what this man has to say.

So, let's listen to him again:

> What I received I passed on to you as of first importance: that Christ died for our sins according to the Scriptures, that he was buried, that he was raised on the third day according to the Scriptures, and that he appeared to Peter, and then to the Twelve. After that, he appeared to more than five hundred of the brothers at the same time, most of whom are still living, though some have fallen asleep. Then he appeared to James, then to all the apostles, and last of all he appeared to me also, as to one abnormally born. For I am the least of the apostles and do not even deserve to be called an apostle, because I persecuted the church of God. But by the grace of God I am what I am (1 Corinthians 15:3-10).

What I want you to notice, members of the jury, is the kind of argument that Paul builds into his statements.

It is not an obvious argument because he is more concerned with reporting than arguing, but it is there, nonetheless. Bear in mind that we are reading old documents, but these statements were originally made to Paul's own generation, to his contemporaries, to those people who were alive when these things happened. To them Paul says important things that we might miss.

For instance, when reporting his experience on the road to Damascus he says that the men travelling with him saw the same bright light that he saw, but did not hear or did not understand the words spoken to him. The implication to his contemporaries is clear: these men are still around—*go and ask them*.

And Paul does something similar in his second statement (quoted above). He talks about the fact that more than five hundred people saw Jesus alive after his death and burial, some of these people have since died, but most of them are still alive. The implication is exactly the same: these people are around the place—*go and ask them*.

Clearly the witness we have before us is a man who is confident that what he is telling is the absolute truth that will stand close scrutiny and rigorous checking. Dismissing out of hand the evidence of such a witness would be a thoughtless and foolish thing to do.

∾

ASSESSING
THE TESTIMONY

In this imaginary 'civil court case' that we are trying—or that you are trying, as a member of the jury—we have now heard from a number of key witnesses. But there is another kind of testimony that I want to bring to your attention, and possibly the best way to do that is to take the stand myself. In fact, I take the stand as an 'expert witness'.

You know what it is like in many trials: experts are called because they have expertise in forensic science, or in medicine, or explaining complicated financial matters, or whatever. I present myself as an expert witness in understanding the difference between fact and fiction. My expertise comes from the fact that I have written both.

As a writer of fiction, I have written 15 novels and more than 50 short stories. In addition, I have written stories (plot lines) for a television drama series (a detective show called *Murder Call*). I have written novels set in my home city of Sydney, and based on my own experience as a host of talk-back radio shows (*Second Death* and *Third Bloodstain*). I have written one novel set at an archaeological dig in Egypt in 1919—based on careful research into both the location and the period. I have written half a dozen short novels featuring the most famous fictional detective of all, Sherlock Holmes (from *The Curse of the Pharaohs* to *Footsteps in the Fog*), keeping my version of Holmes as close as possible to the original created by Sir Arthur Conan Doyle. I have written a horror-fantasy novel entitled *Outbreak of Darkness*—all 120,000 words of it, inspired by the writings of C. S. Lewis (especially his novel *That Hideous Strength*). I have invented characters and incidents and composed dialogue. I have some idea of what it means to tell a fictional story.

At the same time, I also know what it means to report facts. For some thirty years I have worked as a radio and television journalist. Like all journalists, I know that facts have to be checked. There is a well-known saying among journalists: "Opinion is free, but facts are sacred". In other words, hold any opinion you like, express any opinion you like, but check your facts, do your research, make your phone calls—just make sure you have the facts right. I have worked as an editor and executive producer, and I know what it means to edit a script for a news program, or a current affairs program, trying to make the story as clear as possible while sticking carefully to only those facts that have been properly researched and checked and established as facts.

I know what it means to report facts, and I know what it means to compose fiction—and I know the difference between them.

When I go back to these original source documents about Jesus (in the New Testament part of the Bible) I recognize what I find there to be fact rather than fiction.

One of my colleagues once expressed this same idea by saying that reporting has a distinctive 'smell' or 'flavour' or 'feeling' to it. What he meant, I think, is that those of us who have been journalists for a long time simply develop a feeling for reporting. We can read a piece of prose and say, "Ah, yes, that's a piece of reporting", and of another say, "No, this definitely is not reporting". Experience teaches that kind of thing. And those of us who are journalists and who read the Bible regularly are agreed—the biographies of Jesus in the Bible have that about them which causes us to say, "Ah, yes, this is reporting".

Sometimes it is small things, such as sticking in a bit of irrelevant detail. For example, at the end of John's Gospel we find a story about a great catch of fish. Simon Peter, Thomas and a bunch of the others went fishing on the Sea of Galilee. They fished all night and caught zilch. The next morning Jesus appeared on the beach, shouted out a few instructions about where to cast their net, and they immediately hauled in an enormous catch. Various important things then happened, but just in passing, John says this, "Simon Peter climbed aboard and dragged the net ashore. It was full of large fish, 153 of them, but even with so many fish, the net was not torn" (John 21:11).

This detail, of the exact number of fish caught (153), is entirely irrelevant. It doesn't mean anything. There's no reason for it to be there. It contributes nothing to the story. It is there simply because it happened. (And I guess it's the sort of thing Rex Hunt, or any other fisherman, would notice.) And this happens all over the place in the New Testament—small unimportant details are there because what we are reading is eyewitness stuff.

And this same characteristic is repeated throughout the New Testament. There are many small irrelevant details included simply because they happened. This is the kind of thing that says to the experienced reporter, "This is reporting".

Something else needs to be added to what I have already said—namely what is missing.

What I notice as an experienced writer of fiction is that the stories of Jesus lack the neat shape and structure that fictional stories always have. For example, at the beginning of the Gospels the enemies of Jesus have all the political power. At the end of the Gospels those same enemies *still* hold all the political power. If this story was fiction, that would never have happened.

Since Jesus is clearly the hero of the story, any fictional story would have ensured that at the end of the tale his political enemies had been embarrassed and driven from office. Think of all those Hollywood movies you have seen over the years where the hero is the victim of terrible injustice, but heroically fights back. In the end the hero wins, and the villains are exposed as being the true villains that they are.

This is the way fiction works. This sort of thing simply does not happen in the New Testament accounts of Jesus, because they are not fiction—because they stick to the facts. So, those are the kinds of things I can tell you as an expert witness—an expert on the difference between fact and fiction.

And to what I say, we need to add the sort of evaluation of the eyewitness evidence that any jury is called upon to do.

One of the standard text books on this subject is called *Phipson on Evidence*. And here is part of what it says on this subject of evaluating testimony: "The credibility of a witness depends upon his knowledge of the facts, his intelligence, his disinterestedness, his integrity, his veracity. Proportioned to these is the degree of credit his testimony deserves from the court or jury".

The witnesses who say that Jesus came back from the dead seem to fit these requirements.

They are certainly intelligent—we can tell that from the way they wrote. They are people of great integrity and veracity—a fact we can know from the way in which they recorded their own failures and inadequacies so honestly, rather than 'air brushing' them out.

The one issue on which they might be failed is that of 'disinterestedness'. This word simply means being impartial or objective. And there can be no doubt that those early followers of Jesus were far from being impartial. They were convinced that the coming of Jesus, and his conquest of death, was the best news since sliced bread. They were excited about it. They wanted everyone to hear it. So, in that sense, they were not disinterested.

However, in another, more important sense, they were. They had no *personal* interest in the story about Jesus. They had nothing to gain personally from whether you, or somebody else, believed the story or rejected the story. Having the story accepted did not make them richer, and having it rejected did not make them poorer. In fact, by repeating this story they faced persecution, arrest, torture and possible death. They gained nothing from the acceptance or otherwise of the story of Jesus—and in that important sense, their testimony is 'disinterested'.

Furthermore, there is a whole bunch of these people, and the testimony of each one corroborates the testimony of the others. Everything fits together and tells a well-supported, well-evidenced story. They understood the importance of eyewitness testimony, and again and again they said, "We are witnesses to these things" (for example, in Acts 10:39). And the testimony of each eyewitness confirmed and corroborated the testimony of other eyewitnesses.

In the case of the story of Jesus we are standing on solid ground—the foundation is solid fact.

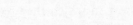

CIRCUMSTANTIAL EVIDENCE

*N*ow, members of the jury, we turn our attention to something called 'circumstantial evidence'. This is the evidence that is derived from changed circumstances. If there is some clear, obvious change in circumstances and that change will fit with one account of what has happened but not another—then that 'circumstantial evidence' is taken as confirming one story and

disconfirming the other.

There are two elements or components in this circumstantial evidence I want you do consider, members of the jury.

The first is the state of the first followers of Jesus immediately after the death of Jesus. When Jesus was arrested, on a Thursday night in the garden of Gethsemane just beyond the walls of Jerusalem, most of his followers fled. Peter (as we've already discussed) followed Jesus at a distance, waited outside the hall where his trial was held, and then denied Jesus and finally fled when he was challenged. Just outside the city of Jerusalem was the small town of Bethany, and, in all probability, that is where most of the disciples fled to (perhaps to the home of Martha and Mary in that town.)

When Jesus died, at the foot of the cross was a small group of women and one young man—so much for the supposedly stout-hearted men who had followed him for three years. One can understand their reaction. Their master had been seized by the authorities, rushed through a mockery of a trial, and then put to death. Clearly anyone who followed him was facing the risk of similar treatment. With Jesus' death, his followers feared for their own lives. They talked about going back to their old professions and trades. The former Galilean fishermen talked about the possibility of returning to Galilee and taking up fishing once more. They were clearly at a loss as to what to do.

They were deeply depressed and grieving over the death of their master, whom they had loved and followed. They were dispirited, defeated, down-hearted—in a word, beaten. That is the first circumstance you need to focus on.

Now shift your focus to the city of Rome, the imperial capital of the mighty Roman Empire, some 30 years later, to the time of the Emperor Nero (who lived from AD 37 to AD 68).

His full name was Nero Claudius Drusus Germanicus, and he became emperor in AD 54. His character quickly emerged, and it was not a pleasant character—his rival claimant to the throne, Britannicus, was poisoned, and Nero's own mother, and his wife, were also put to death. His vanity led him to appear in public as a musician and a charioteer. His passion and cruelty caused him to kick his second wife, Poppea, to death—one crime among many.

In AD 64 there was a great fire in Rome. Many people blamed Nero himself for this fire—gossip suggesting that he burned down much of the city so that he could rebuild it according to his own grandiose plans. In order to shift the blame from himself, Nero chose to blame the Christians—and fiercely persecuted them.

From those two circumstances this question arises: how could those defeated, disheartened, dispirited, small group of people come to be so significant, so noticed, and have such an impact, that a mere 30 years later they could be blamed for the great fire of Rome?

Thirty years is only half a lifetime, but in that half a lifetime those early Christians had turned the Roman Empire on its ear. What was it that changed them? What changed them from being defeated, done, beaten and ready to give up, to people with such fire in their belly that they turned the world upside down, carried the name of Jesus throughout the whole empire, and even the emperor himself had heard of them.

To account for such a change in these disciples requires something dramatic, something huge, something powerful—something like: the resurrection of Jesus from the dead.

MATERIAL EVIDENCE

$\mathscr{N}$ow, members of the jury, let me present you with some material evidence. This is evidence that you can see with your own eyes.

In order to collect this evidence all you need to do is to travel around almost any large city anywhere in the world: in Europe, Africa, the United States, South America, Australia, New Zealand—wherever. What you will notice in most cities is that there are churches all over the place. They are easy to pick, they usually have a cross on the front. From Scotland to Canada, from Nigeria to Russia, from Germany to Argentina: churches are all over the place.

And my point is: they *shouldn't be there*!

The faith founded by Jesus should have died out almost 2,000 years ago. The very name of Jesus should have been forgotten, perhaps known only to a very few scholars who study the remote corners of ancient history.

Why do I say this? Well, stop and work it out for yourself. In the first place, consider the situation of the disciples immediately after the death of Jesus—the situation I sketched about above. There they are: small in number, depressed and grieving, and ready to give up. They should, logically, have given up, and the faith of Jesus should have died out with them.

There is plenty of evidence of religious movements beginning and ending in the ancient world. In the time of Jesus there were a number of movements within Judaism (and remember, Jesus was a Jew, and the faith he founded began *within* Judaism). In the first century in Judea there were the

Sadducees, and the Pharisees, and the Essenes. Where are these movements today? Where are their churches?

Similarly, the world at that time was filled with what we call 'pagan religions'—the worship of Zeus, of Mithras, of Diana of the Ephesians. Where are those religions today? Where are their churches, or temples, or places of worship?

And I've only started to scratch the surface. If you sat down to study first century religious movements the list would be much longer than the few I've mentioned. Out of all those small, new religious movements of the first century, why has Christianity not only survived but spread around the globe, while the rest have died out? How can that be explained?

Judaism was, in the time of Jesus, already several thousand years old and had an entire nation behind it. By way of contrast, Jesus had perhaps 500 followers, and, after his death and burial, they were ready to give up.

How come churches dedicated to Jesus exist in every major city on earth today?

That is a fact that requires some explaining.

The contrast here is with Islam. When Mohammed, the founder of Islam, died in AD 632 he was 62 years of age—Jesus was only about half that age when he died. Mohammed died, peacefully, in his bed, revered as a prophet, leader and ruler. Jesus was brutally executed as a criminal by the Roman authorities. By the time Mohammed died, the religion he had founded, Islam, had tens of thousands of followers. Jesus left behind some 500 followers. At the time of Mohammed's death, Islam dominated the whole Arabian peninsular. The followers of Jesus were tradesmen, businessmen and minor public servants—they dominated nowhere.

The subsequent success of Islam is not surprising—it is exactly what we would expect. The subsequent success of Christianity is astounding—it cannot be accounted for.

Unless, something remarkable happened, as I said above, that changed those first followers dynamically—something with the dynamic power of dynamite, that exploded in their lives and exploded around the world. It would have to have been something utterly stunning and remarkable—something like: the resurrection of Jesus from the dead.

Part 4

CONSIDER YOUR VERDICT

*W*e began this 'trial' by suggesting that the appropriate standard of proof would be the 'balance of probabilities'. And I put it to you, ladies and gentlemen of the jury, that this standard of proof has now been met—that on the balance of probabilities, when all the history, all the testimony, all the evidence, and all the objections, have been taken into account it is reasonable to say that Jesus really did come back from the dead.

It is remarkable, it is astounding, but, on the balance of probabilities, it is also true.

Now, in my final remarks to you as members of the jury, I wish to draw your attention to the significance of this great fact.

A great Jewish scholar named Pinchas Lapide once set out to conduct an impartial investigation into the claims of the resurrection of Jesus. He decided, after considering the same sort of evidence as has been put before you, that in all probability Jesus really was killed, and buried, and then came back to life again. And that's all. He decided it happened, but that it didn't mean anything. That it was just one of those remarkable phenomena that do happen from time to time—like lightning striking the same place two or three times, or like spontaneous human combustion, or like the sinking of the *Titanic*. It was, said Lapide, a remarkable, unexpected, even astonishing thing, but it was just a phenomenon—and it didn't mean anything.

Well, I wish to disagree. As much as I agree with Lapide's examination of the facts, I cannot agree with the conclusion that he draws from those facts.

If Jesus really did come back from the dead, as now seems to be the case, that tells us a number of things.

First, it tells us that Jesus is God. The defeat of death can mean nothing less. Whatever the physical history of the universe, it points to a non-physical origin beyond itself. That which is behind the world is more like a mind than anything else. Jesus is that mind in a human body. That is how and why death was defeated. The universe in which we live is not a 'closed' system, nor is it a chaotically 'open' system: rather it is a 'controlled' system, and Jesus is the eternal being who controls the universe, entering human history in a decisive, interventionist way.

Do you remember the way 'Doubting Thomas' reacted when confronted with the risen, living Jesus? He said, "My Lord and my God". That is the right and proper response. That is the sound of Thomas recognizing Jesus for who he really is. Jesus accepted the worship of Thomas, just as he accepted the worship of others, for he had no doubts about his own identity. And if we ever had any doubts, the resurrection of Jesus from the dead should settle them for us.

Second, Jesus is the judge. That same Paul we met as a witness, stood up in the marketplace in ancient Athens and said that God has "set a day when he will judge the world with justice by the man he has appointed. He has given proof of this to all men by raising him from the dead" (Acts 17:31). When God brought Jesus back from the dead it was, in part, to say to us: here is your appointed judge.

Some people may, at this moment be feeling a little confused. Didn't I say, just a moment ago, that Jesus is God, and now am I saying that God brought Jesus back from the dead? So, which is it? Is Jesus God or is he not? Yes, Jesus is God, but he is not all of God.

There is only one Creator God—God is One and God alone is God. However, from God's revelation of himself in his book, the Bible, we learn that within the one God are three persons.

This is the biblical teaching called 'the trinity'—and it's not easy to understand. Which is exactly what we would expect, isn't it? Any God who was just as comprehensible as we are would not be the great Creator God. The thing that God must be is vastly beyond human beings—beyond our merely mortal standard of power, and intelligence, and understanding. The three 'persons' who together are the one God are, God tells us in the Bible— Father, Son and Spirit. And all three of them are involved in God's great intervention in this world that reached its climax when Jesus came back from the dead.

When we started this case, we said our goal was to discover the truth about Jesus: who he was and what happened to him. We have now discovered a great deal of that. But there is more to be looked at. For instance, Jesus, we have discovered, is judge. This means, among other things, that *we face judgement*.

For the moment you may be in the jury box formulating your judgement, but the day will dawn when you will be in the dock and Jesus will be on the bench passing judgement on you.

The third thing that the resurrection of Jesus means is that forgiveness is available. God's standard is perfection. No flaws are allowed in those God admits to his paradise. Well, it wouldn't be paradise much longer if God allowed imperfect people in, now would it? That means, that at the judgement we all stand condemned because we fail to satisfy God.

The reason Jesus came into this world was because of the just demands of God, and of the just universe he has made, that evil be punished. In fact, he took the punishment that our evil deserves. Jesus died your death, suffered your punishment, and purchased your forgiveness. The judge comes down from the dock, pays your penalty, and forgives your offences. Now that's the sort of judgement I can cope with! And that sort of judgement is what Jesus offers to all who will turn from their way to his way and entrust their lives into his hands. The death and resurrection of Jesus means that forgiveness is possible.

The only entry to heaven is marked 'Forgiven by Jesus'—and the only people who never get to heaven are those who think they don't need to be forgiven by Jesus.

Finally, the fact that Jesus came back from the dead gives us new hope and new life in the face of death. We all die. Physical death is one of the great facts of every human life. And beyond death lies eternity. But where shall we spend eternity? With God, with Jesus, and his people, in paradise? Or proudly rejecting forgiveness at the hands of Jesus—demanding our independence, our autonomy, off on our own, forever? That second prospect sounds to me like sheer hell—which is exactly what it is.

But we can have hope in the face of death if we confess that Jesus is exactly who he claimed to be—God come among us—and that he did exactly what he came to do—died on our behalf and came back from the dead. These things are what the resurrection of Jesus means.

The fact itself is pretty overwhelming.

But, in a sense, the meaning of it all is even more overwhelming.

However, that is no excuse for not doing your duty as a jury member. It is time now to retire to the jury room, to elect a foreman (or should we say "foreperson" these days?) and get on with your deliberations. It is important that you apply the legal standard of proof that we considered in the beginning: the 'balance of probabilities' standard. But it is also important that you go beyond that, and work out what your verdict means for you in your life—both here and now, and in the future, and I do mean the long term future (yes, it's eternity I'm speaking of).

The one thing a jury cannot escape is delivering a verdict. And you *will* deliver a verdict on Jesus whether you want to or not, whether you intend to or not. By simply dismissing this whole thing, and going on living your own life, your own way, without Jesus, without the personal, positive link with the Living God that Jesus offers, just doing nothing, in other words—that is a verdict *against* Jesus. Doing nothing is enough to oppose Jesus. Jesus himself said: "He who is not with me is against me" (Matthew 12:30).

Or you can decide that Jesus is exactly who the resurrection shows him to be: namely the God to whom you owe your allegiance. You can acknowledge God as God, you can serve God as God, by asking Jesus to forgive you, and change you, and take over the running of your life both now and forever.

The one thing you cannot avoid is a verdict—if you refuse to think about Jesus, your daily life will pronounce the verdict for you. So, what will it be? Are you with Jesus, or against him? Do you stand on the side of life? Or on the side of death?

NOTES

The Key Question
C. E. M. Joad's views on Jesus—both as a believer and an unbeliever—can be found in his book *The Recovery of Belief: a Restatement of Christian Philosophy* (Faber, 1952).

In Court
The quote is from Val Grieve's book on the evidence for the resurrection entitled *Your Verdict* (see reference below).

Hostile Witnesses
There are numerous editions in print of both Flavius Josephus' *Antiquities of the Jews*, and Publius Cornelius Tacitus's *Annals* or *Histories*.

The Primary Source
The quote is from J. A. T. Robinson's *Redating the New Testament*, Westminster Press, 1976.

The Counter Argument
Sir Norman Anderson was Professor of Oriental Laws at London University, and then Director of the Institute of Legal Studies. In 1966 he published a small booklet summarising, as its title says, *The Evidence for the Resurrection*. Also relevant is his 1985 book *Jesus Christ: the Evidence of History*.

Among Sir Frederick Kenyon's relevant works on this subject are *Our Bible and the Ancient Manuscripts* (Eyre & Spottiswoode, 1898), *Handbook to the Textual Criticism of the New Testament*

(Macmillan, 1912), *The Story of the Bible* (Murray, 1936) and *The Bible and Archaeology* (Harper, 1940).

Theories

Geza Vermes is best known as the translator of the Dead Sea Scrolls. This quotation comes from *Jesus the Jew: a Historian's Reading of the Gospels* (Collins, 1973).

Explaining the Grave

This account of crucifixion is based on Professor A. Rendle Short's book *The Bible and Modern Medicine* (see reference below).

Time Out to Consider

The case of Dallas County v Commercial Union Assurance Co is cited by Ross Clifford in his book *Leading Lawyers Look at the Resurrection* (see reference below).

A Question of Contradictions

Ross Clifford tells this story in greater detail in *Leading Lawyers Look at the Resurrection*.

Sir Robert Anderson was Assistant Commissioner of Scotland Yard at the time of the "Jack The Ripper" murders. This quote comes from his book *A Doubter's Doubts About Science and Religion* (Pickering and Inglis, 1924).

Consider Your Verdict

The quote is from Pinchas Lapide's famous book *The Resurrection of Jesus: A Jewish Perspective* (Fortress Press, 1983).

BIBLIOGRAPHY

Paul Barnett, *Is The New Testament History?*, Hodder & Stoughton, Sydney, 1986.

Paul Barnett, *The Truth About Jesus,* Aquila, Sydney, 1994.

Paul Barnett, *Jesus and the Logic of History*, Apollos, 1997.

Ross Clifford, *Leading Lawyers Look at the Resurrection*, Albatross, Sydney, 1991.

Val Grieve, *Your Verdict*, InterVarsity Press, Bromley, 1988.

Murray J Harris, *Raised Immortal*, Marshall Morgan & Scott, Basingstoke, 1983.

C S Lewis, *Mere Christianity*, Fontana, 1955.

C S Lewis, *The Problem of Pain,* Fontana, 1957.

C S Lewis, *Miracles*, Fontana, 1958.

Geivertt and Habermas (eds), *In Defence of Miracles*, Apollos, London, 1997.

Josh McDowell, *More Than a Carpenter*, Kingsway, London, 1979.

Josh McDowell, *A Ready Defense,* Thomas Nelson, 1993.

Josh McDowell and Don Stewart, *Answers to Tough Questions*, Alpha, Aylesbury, 1980.

Frank Morrison, *Who Moved the Stone?*, Faber, London, 1958.

Alvin Plantinga, *God and Other Minds*, Cornell University Press, Ithaca, 1967.

Alvin Plantinga and Nicholas Woltersdorff (eds), *Faith and Rationality*, University of Notre Dame Press, 1983.

Hugh Ross, *Creation and Cosmos*, NavPress, Colorado, 1993.

A. Rendle Short, *The Bible and Modern Medicine*, Paternoster Press, London, 1953.

Francis Schaeffer, *Escape From Reason*, InterVarsity Press, London, 1968.

Francis Schaeffer, *The God Who is There*, Hodder and Stoughton, London, 1968.

Richard Swinburne, *The Existence of God*, Clarendon Press, Oxford, 1991.

J. A. Thompson, *The Bible and Archaeology*, Eerdmans, Grand Rapids, 1982.

Ravi Zacharias, *Jesus Among Other Gods*, Word, Nashville, 2000.

Ravi Zacharias, *A Shattered Visage*, Wolgemuth & Hyatt, Brentwood, 1990.

WEBLIOGRAPHY

Answers to Tough Questions
  www.gospelcom.net/rbc/questions

Christianity: Truth or Lie? www.christianapologetic.org

Evidence for God from Science www.godandscience.org

For an Answer www.forananswer.org

Ravi Zacharias www.gospelcom.net.rzim

Reasons to Believe www.reasons.org

Skeptics Welcome www.apologetics.org

Stand to Reason www.str.org

Ten Reasons to Believe www.gospelcom.net/rbc/rtb

The Crossroads Project www.crossrds.org

Unravelling Wittgenstein's Net: A Christian Think Tank www.webcom.com/ctt